DESTINATION

MECCA

Books by Idries Shah

Sufi Studies and Middle Eastern Literature
The Sufis
Caravan of Dreams
The Way of the Sufi
Tales of the Dervishes: *Teaching-stories Over a
Thousand Years*
Sufi Thought and Action

**Traditional Psychology,
Teaching Encounters and Narratives**
Thinkers of the East: *Studies in Experientialism*
Wisdom of the Idiots
The Dermis Probe
Learning How to Learn: *Psychology and Spirituality
in the Sufi Way*
Knowing How to Know
The Magic Monastery: *Analogical and Action Philosophy*
Seeker After Truth
Observations
Evenings with Idries Shah
The Commanding Self

University Lectures
A Perfumed Scorpion (Institute for the Study of
Human Knowledge and California University)
Special Problems in the Study of Sufi Ideas
(Sussex University)
The Elephant in the Dark: *Christianity,
Islam and the Sufis* (Geneva University)
Neglected Aspects of Sufi Study: *Beginning to Begin*
(The New School for Social Research)
Letters and Lectures of Idries Shah

Current and Traditional Ideas
Reflections
The Book of the Book
A Veiled Gazelle: *Seeing How to See*
Special Illumination: *The Sufi Use of Humor*

The Mulla Nasrudin Corpus
The Pleasantries of the Incredible Mulla Nasrudin
The Subtleties of the Inimitable Mulla Nasrudin
The Exploits of the Incomparable Mulla Nasrudin
The World of Nasrudin

Travel and Exploration
Destination Mecca

Studies in Minority Beliefs
The Secret Lore of Magic
Oriental Magic

Selected Folktales and Their Background
World Tales

A Novel
Kara Kush

Sociological Works
Darkest England
The Natives Are Restless
The Englishman's Handbook

Translated by Idries Shah
The Hundred Tales of Wisdom (Aflaki's *Munaqib*)

DESTINATION
MECCA

Idries Shah

ISF PUBLISHING

Contents

Seek not our resting-place upon this earth:
But find it in the hearts of men.

Rumi

CHAPTER I

Gentleman at Large

OCTOBER IN LONDON. Away beyond the Club's terrace a handful of Embankment tramps crouched under the bare trees. I stood by the reassuring radiator and watched them, oddly contrasting with the inhabitants of my little world.

Was their life, huddled on a public bench, panning out as they wished it – as they had thought it would? Was mine, sprawling in a cosy smoking-room, any more productive? I was not sure that either thought mattered so very much, anyway.

Over in the corner some threadbare diehards of club life smoked and muttered over their leisurely pints. Suave, smooth waiters, smiling, hovering, well-groomed, gave our artificial community a superficial air of well-being that I knew from protracted observation to be purposelessly assumed. Every one of the obsequious servants had in reality more spare cash than the spending money that club life allowed many hard-pressed Members, up to their ears in debt. Clubland was doomed in a day when most people outside these walls thought that a club was a place where one danced until the early hours of the morning. "Keeping up with the Joneses" was about all that was left. We were a survival from another time. At least our Embankment neighbors had perhaps come to terms with life. We had not.

What was I? A writer, a traveler – and an outlaw in a sense. It seemed funny how names, labels, associations

1

of ideas – shadows without substance – could capture and influence men's minds, even today. Even today, when colorlessness was the rule.

A writer, say, is respectable. Even if he is almost antisocial, he can be called bohemian. He is a creative worker, or is supposed to be. That is enough. People must have labels. The scramble is to get the right one, and then to hold on to it...

Writers and travelers are knowledgeable men, people to be reckoned with. Thus runs the general impression. A refugee, on the other hand, is something not very nice. He does not fit into any pattern. A refugee writer? Nothing at all. The adjective, then, swallows the noun. Was one an exile, then, or an *émigré*?

I had left certain things behind in the East, and had in turn collected others in the West. Meantime, the tide of life and of events had passed on. Other times, other ways still clung to the mind: a trap for the unwary, like long ceremonial swords that look well but are a curse to wear.

Introspection can go too far, and you do not need me to tell you that. Little more than four years before I had had all I wanted in a material sense. What exile, though, does not say that he was once rich? This case parallels that of the modern reincarnationists, who seem able to identify former celebrities reborn far more easily than humbler folk. I had to find myself, to come to some sort of terms with the world. If tramps could do so, surely I (a sort of wanderer too) could do the same? *Noblesse oblige* is a delicious fantasy: it does not fill the stomach or really quiet the conscience.

Out of a maze of fogged ideas, salient points began to emerge. I had written a good deal, mostly for my own enjoyment. Much of it, too, had been published; and I was now living on that former hobby in deadly earnest. I could not say that I was enjoying the experience, for I did not regard myself as a creative worker. I could not, that is, weave beauty (or anything else) out of mere words and sell them as literature. I would have to sell what I could, where I could, regardless of any budding talents, irrespective of anything but that check. Surprisingly, I seemed to have no grudge against life. My entire thoughts were turned toward action.

I had to get out of this environment, no doubt about that. Clubs and social life seemed to be for those who earned them, or who did not need to earn at all.

I went upstairs to my bedroom, high above the river.

On a chair was my suitcase, and I turned out its remaining contents. A world map, some stones picked up in South America because they seemed to be of interesting shapes and colors: and a camera – Robot f/2.8.

I unfolded the map on the floor, placed four stones on Asia and Africa, and made my plan.

I had been trying to get some newspaper interested in sponsoring me for a trek through unknown Arabia and Africa. If I "went and returned on my own resources" they would "always be glad to see the material." There are always, it seems, dozens of tiresome young men going about London trying to get people interested in things.

I looked at the stones and the places they marked: Mecca, stronghold of Islam, city forbidden to non-Muslims, goal of every Muslim pilgrim. To visit the Shrine here is the duty of all who follow the teachings of Muhammad. Sudan: land of the dreaded Mahdi, of the Twin Niles, ju-ju and the Mines of Solomon. Afghanistan: country of my grandsires, beyond whose southern border lay the unmapped mountain realm of the firebrand Fakir of Ipi, ruler of three million warrior Pathans. And Petra: a city hewn in prehistoric days from the rose-red living rock, rumored cache of a treasure greater even than that of Solomon, son of David, Commander of the Jinn.

There were seven stones. The last three I placed on Syria and Lebanon and Cyprus, the home of Venus.

That was my way: travel, adventure, material for writings, some measure of oblivion and a taste of the East again, even for a year or so.

I rang up an old friend. "Thinking of going to Saudi Arabia? The King has invited you, of course? No? What are your plans, then? Oh, my dear fellow, you can't just *walk*, you know! Best of luck anyway."

I picked up Robot Two-point-Eight, weighed it in my hand. The day before I had been told that there was a lift going on an ex-Naval surplus boat. "Delivery Tangier, old boy, piece of cake. Care to come along?"

When I was planning my Eastern journey in England, and talking to kindred spirits about the idea of seeking out unusual places and writing about them, one thing seemed to be on everyone's lips.

"Old Tony? No, he isn't around any more. Made his pile in Tangier, they say."

"George? Saw him down in Cornwall, tinkering about with boats. Funny thing, but he seems to have taken up yachting in a big way. Was fitting out three ex-Naval jobs there. I suppose he's got customers for them..." "Freddie? Yes, I got a picture card from him postmarked Canaries, of all places. Said he was just cruising with a few friends..." "Tommy? Don't you know? He got a year for smuggling cigarettes from Tangier to Spain. Used to take them to the Canaries, too, in a fast war-surplus sub-chaser or something. Rotten luck, don't you think?"

Pictures and material on smuggling from Tangier, that was an angle. I set about collecting information. Nobody wanted to talk much, but an old school-friend told me that since the war most of the brighter sparks had high-tailed it for the Mediterranean, where fortunes were to be made. "Guns for the Jews and Arabs, old boy. Then refugees out of India and Pakistan. Then cigarettes and nylons into Europe from Tangier. Tangier is the place. Or Villefranche in France."

But I could not get in touch with anyone who had actually been on the Cigarette Run across the Straits of Gibraltar. The nearest I got was slipping a fat tip to a barman in a small West End club, and being told to come back in a week. What I got in exchange was the only clue available, it seemed.

It was a now-tattered piece of paper, which is before me as I write. I have changed the names and jumbled all the details, of course.

"1. J__ M__. Claims to have had experience on a cigarette ship. 'B' Class ML, and formerly war experience in the Indian Army. Present address unknown, but might be contacted through X Bank, Isle of Man.

"2. G__ S__, formerly of St. Paul's House, Woffingham, Devon. Now running Motor Yacht *Boysie*, c/o GPO, Tangier. Has made several trips across the Straits, and is now selling boats to cigarette interests. While awaiting offers for the boats (which he equips and sails out to Tangier), carries out smuggling charters across the Straits and possibly to the Canaries. A strange type of person.

"3. E__. Former shipmate of No. 2, but fell out with him. Is now somewhere in England, trying to raise capital to buy or charter a ship to use for cigarette work. Says he has not so far been able to get anyone to believe in the plan, or else they will not trust him with the £3,000-odd he needs, or maybe they have not got it. He mutinied against his Captain, once, in the Straits.

"4. D__ W__. Went specially to the Mediterranean to study the question. This is his home address (...). Nobody knows where he is now.

"5. J__ P__. He is a useful and ambitious man, and is trying to break with No. 2, for whom he is a crewman. Keeps his eyes open and should make good soon. Present whereabouts: probably with No. 2 (above) in the Mediterranean. Suggest that you look for further information in Tangier."

There was no reply from the various smugglers to whom I wrote as a result of this information. But somehow the word had got round that my knowledge of languages might be useful in the area...

"Delivery Tangier, old boy, piece of cake. Care to come along?"

Twenty-four hours later I was heading toward the Thames Estuary in *Jemima*, the seventy-foot ex-Naval craft that Aubrey was taking out to the smuggling field. Fate, I exulted, seemed to have taken a hand. I had not been forced to part with Robot Two-point-Eight – which I needed for photos. And I was on my way to the East.

Mecca, here I come, even if I have to walk all the way, once I get on Eastern soil...

CHAPTER II

Tangier: Smugglers' Paradise

AUBREY EXPLAINED THE situation in Morocco to me during those long days of lazing in the sun on the way out.

"Tangier is an international zone carved out of Morocco. It is administered by an international commission which is so neutral that it cuts its own throat at every turn. You can do many things legally which would get you sent right to jail anywhere else. And you can get round almost anything if you have the money. Hundreds of people have made their piles taking cigarettes, penicillin – even drugs – into Europe from Tangier."

"But where do you get the supplies?"

"Cigarettes – I wouldn't touch anything else – are imported in the regular way from America. You can import them yourself, if you wish. Most people buy them from importers, though. These are held in bond for reshipment 'somewhere else.' Legally, you can arrive in a boat and buy all the cigarettes you like, and take them across into Spain. If you need faked papers, for any reason, Tangier is the place to get that done."

"And then what?"

"Then you load them on to your ship, take them to Spain, the Canaries or even Italy, and fence them for what you can get. It is seldom less than 50 percent profit, often over 100 percent."

"How do you make the arrangements as to where you will land the cargoes?"

"Well, you can either turn up with your boat and take the fags as freight for an 'agent,' or you can buy and sell on your own account. If you are freighting, all the arrangements are made for you. All you have to do is to be at some spot when instructed, with cargo, and you get your money, after you hand over the fags."

Aubrey explained to me that it was difficult to set up on one's own without considerable capital. After the war a great many ex-Naval types had bought suitable fast boats cheaply, and gone out to Tangier with them to cash in on the boom there.

Then came difficulties. The Spaniards claimed jurisdiction over the sea for a greater distance than the normal three-mile limit. They arrested boats and captains, and this meant bribery to get them out. "Nowadays you can insure in Tangier against seizure by the Spanish Customs."

The smugglers" job was to load quickly at Tangier, make the rapid run to Spanish territory, and transship into small fishing boats or else land the cargo somewhere where the buyer had sent trucks to pick it up. There were snags: pirates had been in action, and consignments had been hijacked. Again, in order to gain speed when pursued, cargoes had sometimes to be dumped. The Spaniards were using German torpedo boats with fast Mercedes engines, and these could be a real danger.

The trade was believed to run into over £10,000,000 a year, and individual cargoes could produce a profit of between £7,000 and £15,000.

Aubrey himself was only going out "on delivery." This meant that he was working for a combine in Tangier which commissioned him to locate suitable boats in England, buy them, have them reconditioned for the job, and bring them out to them. For this he was paid a salary, commission and expenses: plus what he could pick up from the vendor in the boat-buying transaction itself. This way he was doing better than most: because there was simply no risk. What was to prevent a man dealing in boats?

"Trouble is, old boy," he told me, a little sadly, "expenses are high, and the number of suitable boats are few, because they have mostly been sold. The war has been over some time now. I'll be out with the suckers doing the actual runs soon, if I can't think of another angle."

When we arrived at Tangier, the tiny port was teeming with craft. Aubrey was gleefully hailed by several rough, bearded types: "Attaboy Strawberry, one more for the game," or "Reinforcements ahoy!"

We went ashore, to the offices of the smuggling syndicate. The streets were packed with gleaming American cars, gorgeously dressed women with a Beautiful Spy air, Moorish tribesmen, donkeys and peddlers. The population was so mixed that it just wasn't recognizable as anything definite any more.

Anyone can start a bank in Tangier – it is a free currency area. Banks are opening all the time – there were over eighty when I was there. *Nouveau-riche* opulence was everywhere: except where the local Moroccans were concerned. They seemed to have been rather adversely affected by this descent of international capital upon them. Arabs on the whole are the working population – getting paid the equivalent of about £1 per month – and those locals who have tried to copy the international spivs who are so firmly entrenched do not seem to have been particularly successful.

An exception to this rule, however, was to be found in the "Managing Director of the Burnous Import-Export Corporation" – whom I shall call Akram el Burnous – our host and Aubrey's boss.

In the richly furnished offices of Messrs Burnous, the Chief entertained us to coffee, cultured conversation and a display of ready wit.

He was a small, fat man, of some sort of Arab extraction, who spoke a number of languages, and – as he told me – had his suits flown from Savile Row because he was too busy to go over there to be fitted. "One day, perhaps, my friend, I shall be able to retire. Then…" His fingers flashed with diamonds, his round face glistened with holy joy. I would not be surprised if he were worth millions, in any currency you care to mention.

Burnous promised to get me on one of his ships as interpreter. He also warned me that if there was any "incident due to your being associated with us, it will be you that suffers, and that is definite." Now we knew where we stood. Aubrey sounded Burnous on the question of whether he might be allowed to operate a boat if he bought one and came down to Tangier. The boss was in a good mood. "Certainly, of course. I know that things are getting hard in England about the supply of boats. If you can get about three more, then you can come over here. I am trying to get new ones made. You know, these wartime craft are falling to pieces. New ones are very expensive, but the worst thing is the time for delivery. I cannot afford to wait six months. Really, boat-builders are tiresome…."

CHAPTER III

Contraband Runner

IT WAS A moonless night as we hove-to outside the Spanish three-mile limit. Lights out, cigarettes doused, we waited – nerves really keyed up to the limit.

Would it be another case of dumping £20,000 worth of American cigarettes, a wild dash in the converted naval launch from the German-built Spanish E-boats – or yet another triumphant bonus-night, with a week's shore leave and a spending spree in the glittering shops of Tangier?

I was the only passenger aboard. Although I was not paid, and did not regard myself as a smuggler in any sense of the word, I was fully covered by "smugglers" insurance," with compensation clauses and free legal aid, should anything happen.

The Free Traders found that Canary Islands trips were the easiest, as they explained to me during the idle moment of our voyages. At Las Palmas, they said, it was merely a matter of landing the stuff and collecting the money. Nobody seemed to know where the Customs men were – not that they really wanted to know. The snag here was that the profits were small – what economists call marginal. Pay for the crew was less too. But a lazy tour out to the Canaries was considered an essential break for the overtaxed nerves of the contrabandists, now and then.

Several one-night dashes on the "bread-and-butter" run across the Straits from North Africa to Spain had taught me a good deal about such things as security, engine repairs, even navigation. I certainly knew now just how good and how bad my nerves were.

Daily, immense cargoes of the world's goods – nylons, cigarettes, penicillin, even dope – poured in and out of the Tangier Customs sheds. Anyone with the right contacts and enough nerve and capital could buy or charter a fast surplus naval vessel, register her as a yacht and go into business.

Recently, however, as I learned, things had become a little more difficult. The official part of the business, handled by "Agents" (which can mean anything, and generally means stooges for the pseudonymous bosses), was easy enough. Nobody could stop you from sailing out of the harbor at ten at night, loaded to the gunwales with luxury goods which officially neither Spain, France nor Italy could afford to import.

The cigarettes, for example, will have cost the smugglers about sixpence for twenty. They would sell over the water "wholesale" for anything up to one-and-sixpence, or its equivalent in whatever currency the smuggler demands. The sixpenny buying price includes Customs duty (where applicable), import charges and other "expenses." But all cargoes being "In Transit" are out of bond and duty-free. Naturally the ships" papers show your destination to be Samoa or anywhere you care to mention while they are being forged. It is usual, of course, to make the destination appear plausible, and on the return to have documents indicating correct delivery, just in case of inquiries.

Where the real snag comes in is the fact that informers paid by rival gangs, or the police of various countries, keep a very wary eye on cargoes. This means that from the moment the craft is loaded at Tangier the prevention authorities of at least three Mediterranean nations will probably have been alerted, and the boat may be challenged somewhere at sea.

If this snooping were inevitably successful, of course, nary a cargo could get through unintercepted. In actual fact during the autumn "season" as many as twenty outfits may be regularly plying back and forth under cover of darkness.

How is this managed?

It was frequently alleged to me that the Spanish authorities could be "squared." Spurning that unsupported allegation as unworthy of a great Iberian nation, we arrive at the second and third possibilities. Either the Agent from whom one works can rebribe the spy or (which was the general procedure) the boat may be loaded at dead of night, far from any inhabited place. Real, old-fashioned freebooting stuff, this, and not one of the red-blooded men of the new Spanish Main would dream of thinking of himself as anything even faintly resembling a crook.

The Spanish Customs, as already noted, were said not to accept the three-mile limit. My skipper, in common with most of his contemporaries, thought this extremely unsporting. Several boats, he said, had been blown out of the water for failing to stop and account for themselves, when they were found cruising by night four or five miles from Spain. This generally happened when they were overloaded, and could thus not achieve the necessary evasive action. It was believed that those boats which carried reasonably light cargoes, with engines in good order, were never caught.

A "Fairmile" type of craft can make enough speed to show a clean pair of heels to even *E*-boats, providing that she is light or can be unloaded double-quick. For this reason, cargoes were sometimes carried on deck, roped and tarpaulined, every man drilled in his split-second emergency role. "It is no fun at the actual moment of crisis," Aubrey told me, "but there is something exquisite about the memory. Just try hurling overboard 850 cases of cigarettes in a matter of a couple of minutes and zigzagging frenziedly the while to escape the merciless Spanish searchlights, if you want to know what it is to be good and scared."

On this particular night the Captain got away with it. Promptly at 3 a.m., a small Spanish fishing boat loomed out of the blackness. Signal lights blinked cautiously. All was well. This was not to be a "run in" but a transshipment: far easier, though less well paid. Legally, according to our advice, we were completely covered, for we were operating outside the internationally agreed limit.

The Spanish Agent, looking like a film version of a highly successful Yankee businessman, came on board. The American skipper of our outfit (who said that he had "forgotten" to return to his Army unit when it was stationed in Italy) pulled a half banknote out of his pocket. Another half was produced by the Agent. They fitted, numbers were the same. We all smiled. No trap here... unless...

A horrible moment came when a light airplane equipped with searchlights buzzed around. A coastguard. The two parties on our craft glared at one another, mutually suspecting. But we bore no lights, and neither did the Spanish fisherman. The "enemy," ignorant and unheeding of our blasphemous curses, slipped back toward the coast of Spain.

We went below, and I counted out the money. Sixty-six thousand dollars in American notes. On deck the crew, casual and efficient through months of experience, transferred the cases – nearly 9,000 cartons of 200 cigarettes each – into the rowboats of the Spanish ship.

Within an amazingly short time, three faint whistle-blasts told us that the job was done.

By the next afternoon – taking a wide detour and heading back from an entirely different direction – we were in Tangier again.

A total stranger stopped me in the street that evening and muttered in a broad Scottish accent that he heard that I had been with the Blue Bonnets over the Border. I knew that there was probably not a soul in the smuggling fraternity who had not heard of the successful run.

At one time the muscling-in of American gangsters brought out a particularly ugly side of Tangier life. At first there had been something of the old-fashioned grace of gentlemen adventurers about the smuggling community. Then, out of the blue, the Italian-Americans in their expensive boats started a kidnapping and hijacking regime which forced smaller operators entirely out of the game. The loss of a single cargo, if one is making a way up the steep scale of plowed-back and re-plowed profits, can mean complete financial ruin.

One load lost and several months may have to go by before really economic returns are again reached. Chased by the Italian Customs not far from Genoa, our Skipper once dumped overboard more than twenty thousand pounds" worth of smokes and penicillin. In order to make up for these losses, he had to plow back every penny of profit from six potboiling trips to the Canaries.

The biggest figures behind smuggling in Tangier are, as I have said, anonymous. In some cases this means that their connection with smuggling cannot be proved. Their organization is composed of a series of broken links, with nobody knowing more than is good for him.

As a general rule, skippers pick their own crews and give their final operational orders three or four hours before loading-time. When the crew reports, the goods are already on the quay awaiting checking and stowing, with shipment papers in order: or, at least, watertight.

The ambition of every skipper is to become his own boss, to have his own boat, and eventually to settle down to a less harrowing life.

Information that I collected in Tangier, however, indicated that only about one in five of the inexperienced venturers who simply bought a boat and headed for the smugglers" paradise actually succeeded. The rest either were drowned, disappeared, died in gang fights when the American gangsters were still there, were captured by the Customs of one country or another: or lost their cargoes early on and had to start all over again from the beginning. It takes a good deal of self-discipline and luck to be a successful smuggler. The effect of vast amounts of easy money on most of the smugglers who did strike lucky seemed almost to unhinge them. They were like men from another world.

Our own captain was one who had once brought out his own boat and had lost the cargo on an overloaded run, and was now working for the Boss. He had signed on at Villefranche, on the French Riviera, as a deckhand on a British-manned craft. Rumor had it that he had worked his way up to captain aboard one of those perhaps mythical boats said to have been manned by a band of British ex-Wrens. In any case, he had made dozens of trips, had been inside a Spanish jail, and had had his cargo confiscated several times. He was now climbing the weary stairway to "all or nothing at all."

I had collected my information, but would have tarried a little longer in the fabulous international city, had I not been aching to get moving Eastward. What made me make tracks for Gibraltar in a hurry and away from it all was the rumor that the Captain had contracted for a dope-running trip to Genoa.

Like most people, I am opposed to the drug traffic on almost every ground I can think of. In all fairness to the smugglers it must be said that hardly any of them would handle dope.

As I write this, my thoughts wander to the silent, plush blue of a moonless Mediterranean night. How many skippers that I know – and their crews – are scanning the darkness, engines off, waiting for... a burst of machine-gun fire, perhaps?

Or are they all already in jail?

Gibraltar was the quickest way out. Even here, though, there was unease and a sense of anticlimax. I had hoped to travel eventually to Arabia via French Morocco and Libya. Diverted by visa-trouble, I decided to make for Marseilles, to catch a *Messageries* ship for Alexandria.

SMUGGLERS" PROSPECTUS

This document, better than anything I could write, gives the picture of the Mediterranean contrabandists and their ways. It was prepared by a group of "operators" who had decided to return to Europe in an attempt to buy their own boat and thus cash in on the huge profits of the Tangier Run:

Mediterranean Trade – Tangier to Spain

Summary. Subject of Proposition: cargoes of American cigarettes carried by sea from Tangier to Spain.

Profits to be Expected. On the basis of actual "runs" now in regular operation – private cargoes (owned by the owners of boats) about £15,000 per run, in US$ Freight, carried on behalf of Combines already working there, upward of £2,000 per run. Calculated on a basis of 1,000 cases of cigarettes per cargo.

Culpability in British Law. Nil. No British law is infringed. There is no infraction, either, of international law, in the case of cargoes being transshipped outside the three-mile territorial limit bordering Spain. Tangier implications: none. It is permitted to import cigarettes into Tangier and export them seawards *via* private transport.

Investment Needed. To buy a suitable ex-Naval ship, with a speed of thirty-knots-plus: about £2,500. Alternatively, to buy a suitable MFV or HDML in this country and take it out to Tangier: £1,500. Some MFVs might be available at about £1,000. Buying a share in an existing ship (now being fitted out for operations) in England: about £1,000. This latter figure represents a participation equal to about one third of the profits.

Further details will be found below:

Brief Summary of the position and implications up to date

A very large market exists for American-made cigarettes in France, Spain, Canary Islands and Italy. Currency restrictions – dollar shortage – make this demand insatiable by orthodox methods. The recent war has developed among the local people a taste for American cigarettes: and, in addition, their own government monopoly brands are in most cases greatly inferior.

There is also the large market for foreigners traveling through and resident in Mediterranean lands. At present legally only token imports are permitted in the above-mentioned territories.

A notable exception to this import ban is Tangier: the International Zone on the Moroccan coastline, just across the Straits from Spain and Gibraltar. This is a Free Currency Area: meaning that goods can be imported into Tangier and paid for in US and exported from there to any country by almost any means.

Modus Operandi
(1) Types of Operation

Two main types of trading are to be distinguished: synchronized deliveries arranged by Tangier Agents (combines), who give yacht-owners their cargoes and instructions in Tangier, and arrange for the ship to be met by fishing vessels outside the three-mile limit; and secondly, the independent yachtsmen who buy their own cargoes and make their own selling arrangements for delivery and selling. This report is mainly concerned with the former type of operation.

(2) Typical Operations

In a typical transaction, the procedure is generally as follows. The captain or owner of the boat arrives in Tangier. It is essential that he be known and trusted locally. He makes contact with the Combines, through one or other of their agents. A cargo is arranged by this agent. When the Agent has satisfied himself that the ship is of the kind which is used by his Combine (they have inexplicable caprices about this sort of thing, and have to make sure that certain kinds of engines are fitted, and so on), the cargo is ordered by the Agent, and delivered aboard the ship.

The cargo may be large or small. In the case of a new ship, Agents generally send only a few hundred cases, and also a representative on board, just to see how the thing is "settling down" to work.

Everything is very highly organized. The ship sets sail under cover of darkness, on moonless nights, to make its rendezvous on the other side. The skipper has received half his freight charges in advance, and gets the balance on delivery, in cash.

He is paid in US$6 or more per case, or a total of £2,000. Out of this, the crew of three are paid £20 a week on the average, and a bonus of over £10 for each cargo delivered. Fuel costs 1s. 4d. per gallon (diesel oil), and about 30 gallons are used in the crossing.

Frequency of Operations

It is possible to carry out three to four crossings per week. Delivery to the Canaries, Italy, etc., is paid for at a higher rate. It is possible to insure against mishaps, engine faults, or loss of cargo or boat.

Personnel

The present team proposing this operation consists of the following: one captain, with a two-year record of successful deliveries without mishap; and three assistants, one of whom is skilled in navigation, another in engines, and the third as general hand plus navigator. All personnel can double as deckhands and steersmen.

This team is referred to as The Group. They propose starting as soon as humanly possible, and to that end need a boat. They have all the experience and skills, but lack capital.

The Group proposes that an investor or a group of investors purchase a boat of suitable type, as their contribution, and register it as a yacht. The Group undertakes to sail the boat to Tangier, to make all arrangements, and to begin operations. Profits will be divided – either as follows, or after consultation. No salaries to be paid, entire project to be profit-sharing. Boat to be in the name of the owners or a nominee or the Group. This is immaterial, but the Group wishes to exclude the possibility of suspicion that they will themselves dispose of the boat, or otherwise take advantage of the factual possession of it. Profits to be calculated as net profits, and 75 percent for the Investor(s), with the balance of 25 percent to the Group. Fund to be set up for purchase of additional boat.

Actual plan of operations

Initially, until there is sufficient liquid capital available for the Group to run their own cargoes, owned by themselves, the boat will transport cigarettes for one of the Combines, in the form of freight. This will be about 1,000 cases at £2 per case of 10,000 cigarettes, or a gross return of £2,000 per trip.

Reckoning on four trips a week, the profits will work out at £8,000 per week, less fuel, etc. Within a few weeks, however, the Group would intimate to the Combine's agents that the capacity available for freight had diminished: and less and less freight and more and more cargoes of the Group's own cigarettes would be transported, bought directly from the importers in Tangier, and sold through the Group's own Agents in Spain.

Working on the above figures, it will be seen that a private cargo (i.e. one owned by the Group) being worth up to £15,000, the gross profits could be as high as £15,000 a week. Cigarettes sold in this way are, therefore, a much better investment than the freight flat rate of £2 per case.

This is an exact parallel of operations which have been carried out by British and American crews from 1946 until today, and the overall picture has changed little during that time.

The entire Riviera and the North African coastline from Casablanca to Villefranche is dotted with retired British and American (and other) nationals, who have retired from the smuggling trade after making £100,000 or more. This is one reason for the continual demand for good boats and trustworthy crews. "Retirements" are very common. Being plain businessmen, the Combines cannot bind the smuggling crews to them legally or otherwise after they have made their "pile."

Urgency of immediate action

Apart from the natural desire to commence operations soon, in order that the profits should come in as soon as possible, there are other reasons for speed. Among them may be mentioned that September to October are the times when smuggling always receives an added impetus in the Mediterranean. It is necessary to make arrangements with the Agents, so that they will know what cargo capacity one is providing; and, indeed, that our Group will be in operation at all. Secondly, if we are to participate in the boat which is actually in process of being bought now we must act quickly. This will limit our investment, and get us into operation at the earliest possible date. Most important, there are rumors that a movement may be afoot soon to seek the United States Government's action to limit cigarette exports to Tangier. If this were to happen, the entire smuggling trade would be wiped out at a blow. So we must work fast. We may have only about three months in which to harvest the situation.

Note

The Group is prepared to negotiate on the basis of this Report. It is emphasized that the Group does not seek any liquid capital to be paid in cash to them. They are prepared to take any investor(s) to the spot in Tangier, or Spain, to satisfy themselves that this is a serious and practicable business.

CHAPTER IV

Eastward to Egypt

THE STREET WAS wide, the fire brigade was marching gloriously by, no doubt for the best of reasons. Marseille lay bathed in watery sunshine. One whole day to wait for the ship to Egypt; Tangier seemed a million miles away. I sat in a shaded café terrace: and the waiter brought me – Zimba Kola. I asked him why. "All Spaniards drink Zimba, *m'sieu*." So I drank.

Now here was a touch of mystery. Was this a password? Did I speak French like a Spaniard? Or was the man just a complete dolt, saying the first thing that came into his head? A very French-looking couple came in, and carried on an animated discussion in the most Parisian of accents. Tensely I watched. Yes, they were being served with Zimba all right. Imperiously, they ordered espresso coffee. The waiter retreated, scowling.

So this was Marseilles. Very well, I would investigate further. I would be the mysterious Spaniard, here on important business. I would play the game to the end. I even shouted *Caramba!* very loudly. The waiter scurried up, polishing a glass in the approved manner. For a moment I felt a bit foolish, but the pose was asserting itself. "*Gracias*," I told him, and slapped down a fifty-franc note.

"October in Marseilles," I told myself, and slouched out. As I walked through the shadiest quarters, trying to sense contacts with anyone and everything interesting, I began to realize that *I* might be the most sinister object in sight.

Nobody offered me a doped cigarette, or even a run across to Tangier. I saluted strange-looking Arabs, who smiled back without a word about white slaves. True, one rather flashy youth badgered me for dollars, but I had none to exchange at the very favorable rate being offered.

I spent most of the day looking for photogenic fishermen, and again inspected Hitler's immense Mercedes, which I had already seen on show in England.

"Marseilles," said an Englishman who lived in the same small hotel near the sea, "has been described as a place whose avoidance is in itself an achievement."

I told him that it all depended upon what one wanted out of life. After that, I really began to like the place a little better myself. Here, at any rate, one could buy any quantity of really first-class fruit at low prices, sit or walk in the sunshine, go for a trip in painted boats to the famed Château d'If – and remember that this was the threshold of the Orient. I found no copy here for any of those papers which like to feed their readers on tales of "sinister Marseilles." As I watched one seemingly endless line of infantry marching past, *en route* to Indochina, I thought of these men and their fate. It seemed odd that vice and crime had a greater fascination for many readers than history in the violent making in the Far East.

Somehow the time passed, and I could go on board the ship. In any case I was not here to study France, and even the period on board could be little more than a time for thinking out the problems of getting to Mecca, performing the Pilgrimage, getting pictures – and getting out.

As I arrived at the docks and opened my bags for the Customs official, he pointed dramatically at my dispatch case. In it were nothing more than several packets of enlarging paper ("Do Not Open Except in the Dark"), and what he saw as a decidedly sinister-looking ampoule of developer.

Neither of these things would be opened, I was informed, if I would pay two hundred francs on each. The logic of it was beyond me, and I refused.

A porter was deputed by the exquisitely uniformed *Douanier* (who stood aloof while my feeble mind was grappling with the details) to explain, that, therefore, my hand-baggage would be exempted from search, as a favor.

"At the same time, *m'sieu*, in order to spare yourself needless delay in the opening of the *other* articles, it would be best to pay twenty-five francs each: that will be... two hundred francs."

This beat me. I paid. The bags were chalked: a *douanier* is as good as his word. As the official disappeared toward the nearest bar, the porters, as one man, winked and smiled affectionately, lifting an imaginary glass.

After that I cursed my luck for not having some desperately dutiable contraband with me. It was just as well that I had not, for I was treated with offended aversion by the Egyptian Customs when I eventually arrived there.

I got aboard the ship easily enough: in fact, too easily – without passport or ticket, which I had laid down in the confusion of the douane shed. Now I found that all my attempts to go ashore again were met with the gravest suspicion by everyone I approached to prevail upon the gangway sailors to let me by.

The ships of this line may not have the best possible food aboard, but none can deny that the fittings are luxurious. As usual, the dazzling figure in braid and the neatest of uniforms is just a minor functionary – not the captain.

Literally hundreds of porters – all, so far as I could see, Arabs – were loading oil drums with block and tackle into our holds.

One, the "Captain of Porters," now too old for active work, reclined on a pile of sacks by the quay, reverently placed there for him by a disciple. The Eastern patriarchy seemed strangely out of place. And yet was it? There was something so monotonously hypnotic about the rhythmic chant of the small, lithe men, so unendingly recurrent were the shapes of standard-sized drums, seen in all their shapes and combinations, there on the sling, so bright and silver in the true Mediterranean light, that my mind seemed to tire of taking photographs. Arabs. Oil drums. Oil. Porters. Old Baghdad. The panorama of the years – never far from the oriental mind – seemed to flash through my brain. Leaning on the rails there, in this twentieth century, with thoughts of Aladdin's lamp, of the New East reinvigorated by petroleum, I let myself fall into that state of mind which I suppose Western psychologists would call auto-suggestive escapism, or something like that.

"The trouble with you people," an English professor friend had said to me once, "is that you do not know which century you are living in. To you, Saladin or Suleiman the Magnificent are as real as anyone alive today. And I can prove it." He had gone on to tell me, I reflected, that the majority of Eastern languages had nothing except direct speech: "'I am here,' said Alexander," is an example. It is not possible to say: "Alexander said that he was there." This, the Professor had maintained, was due to the fact that the speaker wanted the events related to be as near as possible; did not want them to appear so old: liked to feel that they had only just occurred, or were still happening.

When we set sail, I spent much of my time at first watching the victorious Egyptian wrestlers and weight-lifters, who were returning home from The Hague, exercising on deck. I often saw their manager – himself once a world champion – coaching

26

them. They were an extraordinarily assorted lot, physically speaking. Some with the characteristically almost Negroid big heads and curly frizzy hair of Lower Egypt; others small, wiry and sensitive-faced, like the Arab; some of the common Mediterranean type that is called Alpine or Latin in Europeans, and Levantine elsewhere. This was something which had a bearing upon another problem which I had set out on my journey to analyze: to what extent can the Middle Eastern peoples be divided into distinct nations? Is their patriotism of the same nature as Western nationalism? Having regard to the fact that most of such peoples have no tradition of independent statehood stretching beyond two or three decades, are they nations at all, in the generally understood sense of the term?

The answer to my first musings, as I had watched the oil drums, came before the nationality question. In the dining-room I sat next to a rosy-cheeked priest, bound, in the complicated itinerary, for the Congo. He talked incessantly across me to a morose, black-bearded character, who, when he did speak more than a monosyllable, seemed always to say: "When I was Mayor of Ranigette!..." I changed places with him. This brought me face to face with the tall, sheikhly figure, who never spoke at all. Like me, he passed his wine to the priest, so I took him for a Muslim.

The eighteen hours before we got under way was a period of continual din and shouting. Roaring forth the monotonous cries of their trade, the Arab stevedores were bringing more and more oil drums to the quay with a speed and dexterity which was almost frightening. Presided over by the aged burnoosed patriarch, they seemed oblivious of anything else. A nod from their chief, the slightest gesture, and the teams, together numbering some two hundred, responded with complete coordination.

Every two hours or so, when they had a short break, one or another brought a water-pipe and mint tea to their leader. All first kissed his hand and then their own.

This little cameo amused me, and I thought I could make a little picture-series of it. I had decided rather precipitately to go to Mecca, but since I left England there had not been much chance to familiarize myself with the rapid-action camera that I had chosen for the job.

I watched the ceremonies and activities of the workers, decided that I would develop my films on the ship, so that if the results were not good enough, I could always buy another camera in Cairo if this one proved defective or unsuitable in any way. Innocent enough. But we were no longer in England. There is a sensitivity in the Mediterranean lands that someone from Britain, accustomed to free and easy ways, has to re-learn.

I had taken about twenty pictures in rapid succession when I felt a hand on my arm. A blue-bereted, typical bourgeois Frenchman stood beside me. "There are so many finer things to photograph in France," he said, "a man of your obvious refinement could picture beauty, rather than those sordid Arab workers. They are not of France: they work here only seasonally, like the carpet-peddlers." He did not seem at all convinced when I tried to explain that, on the contrary, I thought it a pleasing sight that this little social unit maintained its own customs here. Being somewhat impatient by nature, his shrugging shoulders annoyed me. "In any case, is it not something that you French allow them to come here, to live their own way of life? And as to your remark about my supposed refinement... I have never set eyes on you before, let alone talked to you, so you have no idea what my intellectual or other attainments are, any more than I have of yours. And I am content, *m'sieu*, to remain in such ignorance of you."

Next morning at breakfast this man pointed me out in a loud voice to a group of his compatriots as a dangerous anarchist or something similar.

Two days were to pass before I first got to grips with the mind of the East again. As I mused at the rails, staring out to sea, a voice addressed me from behind: "Peace upon Thee," in Arabic. "*Aliakum as-Salam*" ("on Thee Peace also") I said.

Like something out of a medieval story, my Arab vis-à-vis at mealtimes bowed and spoke with dignity. "You bear a famous name, my brother: I have seen it on the passenger-list. I, too, am of the Prophet's clan." He was of the old school. "Let me tell you a story – it will introduce us.

"Thirteen centuries ago our ancestor Muhammad, son of Abdullah, of the mighty Koresh Clan, wiped infidelity and polytheism from pagan Mecca. In its place, as you know, he installed monotheism, and the Worship of the One True God." I bowed. It is customary in Muslim circles to start from a known beginning, developing your theme from remote history down until the present day, if necessary.

"The infidels, plus Romans, Greeks and Egyptians, fell, humbled by the sword of truth and the preaching of bedouin faith. The power of Islam swept westward, led by the conqueror Tarik, after whom Gibraltar – *Gebel-Tarik* – is still named. A relative of Muhammad, the mighty Tarik reached Morocco, the Farthest West known to us. Plunging his horse into the foaming Atlantic breakers, he brandished his sword aloft. 'O Allah, in Thy Name, if there be land beyond this sea, I shall conquer it, bearing witness to Thy Unity and Omnipotence.'"

There was fire in the old man's eyes, his mind visualizing the scene as though it had taken place but yesterday.

"I am directly descended from that man! Your ancestor, the Emperor Musa Kazim the Hashimi, of the Prophet's house, was driven eastward, and his progeny settled in Ajam:

the lands of Persia, then Afghanistan, where they became
lords and warriors. Infidelity reigned in Baghdad, but still the
Muslim armies poured into Spain, overthrowing the Vandals,
the Isbanyol and Kastiliyin. On the mighty ranges of the
Pyrenees, the Sayed, my ancestor, stood, at the head of his
heroes. They looked down from the barren rocks, into the fair
green lush fields of France. 'On, to the conquest of the world,
for Islam!' – thus shouted the captains. The Sayed turned his
horse, and trod slowly away. 'No. We shall remain in Spain.
France is too green,' he said. 'My men would degenerate in
that soft climate: too green, too green,' he said. Thus it was
that we gave time to Charles Martel to gather his forces: and
the Moors were swept from Spain in the end.

"My family returned. They were one of the very few who
escaped the Inquisition. Today they call me a Libyan. I live
on a strip of land between the Sahara and the Mediterranean
Sea. See how we are scattered, we progeny of the lords of
Arabia: the nobility is no more..."

I was to find out that this mentality, the fusing of many
ideas, is typical of Muslims today. In that man's words were
all the elements that are firmly believed in the Middle East:
the invincibility of Muslim arms; reverence for the Prophet's
family and – a key to my pet problem of nationality – the lack
of *national* partisanship on the Western model. You may be an
Arab or a non-Arab; a Baghdadi or a man from Bokhara: but
you are only in a secondary sense an Iraqi, or even an Egyptian.

Saadi, the greatest Persian poet, reflected this in his
writings. "*Harmulkmulk-i-ma'st,ki mulk-i-Khuda-i-ma'st*"
("Every country is my homeland that is God's country"). And
this, in a thousand ways, I was to discover, stems from the
essentially Islamic basis of nationalism in the Middle East.
Western nationalism and political theory, as I had seen it,
sprang from Socrates and Plato, from Marx and Rousseau,
from rationalism allied to the natural affection of one whose

soul is not so dead as not to recognize his native land. Muhammad, on the other hand, strove always to widen the circle of Islam, to include the believers as a nation, rather than as a religious community in the theological sense. One reads in the histories of Islamic expansion of the "Conquest of the Unbelievers," rather than the conquest of Persia, or India. This, to me, brought home again and again the reason why Islam has not lost its grip upon people in the way and to the extent that other religions have lost supporters: Islam has never set out to be a religion, in the same sense as these other creeds.

It was by recognizing this fact that Jamaluddin El-Afghani became, in the nineteenth century, the Middle East's apostle of liberation and patriotism – while yet repudiating nationalism. Today almost every single party or group, from Morocco to Java, claims him as its inspiration, however different their aims. I shall speak of him and his work later, in dealing with his spiritual successors as I came across them. A very great deal of nonsense has been written about the so-called "Panislamic Movement": much of it by orientalists who should know better. This is one fact which my journeys in Egypt and beyond amply proved.

Flags were flying, motorboats sporting a thousand fluttering pennants cruised madly round the ship, as tens of thousands of paid and unpaid supporters of the Egyptian athletes welcomed their heroes at Alexandria harbor. Bow after bow they took, dressed especially in their tracksuits and sunglasses. Every minute the crowds thickened and became wilder; music mounted in frenzied tempo that I could not but feel – uncharitably, I suppose – must be maintained at that pitch only because the players were "high" with hashish. Amid garlands and bouquets, through ranks of pashas three deep, and braving the batteries of cameras, the team stepped ashore, to be chaired to their waiting banquet.

It was morning, and the Cairo train did not leave for a few hours. We landed, to put off time before the departure of the desert express. The least said about Alexandria, perhaps, the better. The Khedive Muhammad Ali is reported to have said, "Egypt is now a part of Europe." It certainly did not seem at first sight to be a part of the East. The heat, of course, was there: so were the flies, and the usual drifting proletariat shabby in its pathetic imitations of Western garb, looking thoroughly dispirited, which it is, and should be. Too many indifferent orientals seemed to have been turned into bad replicas of Europeans. The typical long *galabiyah* or nightshirt which is considered standard fellahin dress is elegant in comparison with a pair of stained dungarees and a tenth-hand topee. These characters were most in evidence in the streets. Garish stalls sold at enormous prices things that one would throw away in England. Broad, sweeping avenues, built with a complete lack of taste, formed concrete jungles, where the heat battled with cement-dust for first place as indigenous pest.

Sadly, I drank an American soft drink in the baroque bar of the largest hotel, where befezzed men-about-town dangled their gold-topped canes and dusted patent-leather brogues (what taste) with silk handkerchiefs. A policeman, politely enough, saluted me and asked for a tip. I gave him five piastres – a shilling – and he seemed content.

There are some good beaches at Alexandria, where the capital's *élite* repair in summer to enjoy themselves. Huge American cars purr through the streets. A little outside the town's center His Majesty King Ahmed Zog, Monarch of All the Albanians, lived in lonely splendor, attended only by an entire Cabinet, who followed him to this immense Riviera-type villa of his exile. One of my first impressions was the amazing depths to which Arabic has sunk as the language of the country. Still, it is always interesting to see what people can do with things: and what the Egyptians have done to Arabic may be noted almost as an example of human ingenuity.

It is no exaggeration to say that if one spoke the literary kind of Arabic which is the day-to-day tongue of the Arabian Peninsula, scarcely a soul in Alexandria would understand it. Before long I had, even in Cairo, to seek literature graduates from Al-Azhar University with whom to practice real Arabic.

In spite of the fact that they feel themselves to be the natural leaders of the Arab world, the Egyptians often unbosom themselves to friends about their un-Arabishness. Their detractors, of course, call them Africans, and they do not like that "one bit" is more American. Many Egyptians feel that in some mysterious way the hand of imperialism must have caused all the evils or disadvantages from which they suffer.

This story is related with relish by Egyptians, who seem immune to its implications for themselves. It is said that a British consular official was greatly alarmed at the headway which French was making in the land of the Nile. Lord Curzon, as he was passing through Cairo, was approached by this functionary. The British community, he said, besought His Lordship's aid in popularizing English. Curzon is credited with having made a typical answer. "French is good enough for the Egyptians!"

Alexandria, I reflected, was no place for me. Cairo was the gateway to Arabia...

CHAPTER V

New Arabian Knights

A THOUSAND YEARS ago and more, the Caliph Haroun-el-Rashid haunted the streets of imperial Baghdad nightly in disguise, seeking to know the true state of affairs among his people. Readers of the *Arabian Nights* will recall that in this way many plots against the Throne were discovered, deserving subjects were eventually rewarded, and the disloyal were rightly chastised, as behooves a well-rounded story.

One of the drawbacks that a traveler and adventurer suffers from when he also writes is that this *sine qua non* of persuasive fiction is often absent. You either arrive on the scene at the end of the last act, or blunder into something in the middle, and probably get ulcers wondering what the end of the whole thing will be.

Of all places, Cairo gives one that feeling of something either completed (like the Arabization of the country ten centuries ago) or in the melting-pot – like the Arab League, the Westernization or the banishing of illiteracy.

Cairo is supposed to be a sink of iniquity, a place of intrigue, plot and counter-plot, headquarters of dope or white slave rings: a thousand and one aspects of shady life and sin. It is easy to talk of these things, easier still to imagine dire deeds and frightful plots amid the medley of rich and poor, mosques and racecourses, palaces and night-clubs, that are the impact upon a casual visitor. But where are these things to be found?

The answer is that, in nine cases out of ten, even if you live in the city for a hundred years, you will not find them. There is one exception to this rule. As with many another thing, like a strange trick of fate, you may stumble across something odder than a hashish-smoker's dream – when you are not looking for it.

And this is just the reason that I found myself meeting the Great Assassin, Haroun, with four hundred million souls as his potential subjects, and probably a pretty strong case of paranoia.

If you do not believe a word of this story, nobody can blame you. All I can say is that every syllable of it is true and leave it at that.

I was dressed in my Arab robes – white headcloth bound with twin gold circlets, and a flowing black *Mishla*, in the Old City, taking photographs of the oldest university in the world: Al-Azhar, "the Resplendent."

After offering the customary two *Raka* (obeisances) in prayer within the immense carpeted mosque, I had risked a rapid snapshot of the entrance from within the precincts, and then wandered down the ancient market where the "genuine" brass bowls of Birmingham lay displayed beside cloth from Japan, rosaries of Mecca, or elephant-stamped incense of India.

I have a weakness for Afghan sandals. Here, far from his native glens, I found a compatriot presiding over his leather stall: and sandals decorated with gold-thread patterns, semi-precious stones and even ivory. Now the Afghans, as any Middle Easterner will tell you, are clannish and a little boastful. Yielding to the impulse, I shouted out the name of the owner which was displayed, like some precious text, upon a gracefully written plaque above the open shelves:

"Aslam Khan, Long Live Afghanistan! May you never be poor!"

Invited into the shop, I drank innumerable cups of green-leaf tea, and we talked of Kabul, of the mountains and the fruits, of the passes and ravines. He had been one of the supporters of Bacha-Saqau, the brigand-king of Afghanistan during the early 1930s. Forced to flee upon the bandit's downfall, he had settled in Cairo, after making the Mecca pilgrimage. Since that time, much had happened: Afghanistan was a settled, progressive state. He had made his peace with the Government, and every three or four years would return home. But business here was good. Sometimes he yearned for the cool, crisp air, the green of the conifers, the clean icy waters of the mountain torrents, but business was good in Egypt...

As we talked, I told him of some of my wanderings, of my search for the unknown, of the wander-bug in general.

Then a customer came into the shop, and Aslam left me with his handwritten manuscript of Khushal-Khan, poet-hero of the borderland. I was immersed in the staccato rhythm of the Pushtu language when Aslam hurried back to me.

"Do you know Persian well? I suppose you must; mine is very bad, because, as you know, I'm a Khyber hillman. Come and help me with this customer, who seems to be a man of substance, and doesn't know Arabic well."

I went forward. The visitor was well over six feet tall, dressed in European clothes with a gold-headed stick, and carried a green rosary in his left hand. By his features I took him for a Kurd – and he spoke Persian like one, too.

"Peace upon you."

"And upon you, and the blessings of Allah!"

"Are you the owner of this shop? I cannot make this man understand Persian, and I must have some shoes made."

"No, I am just a visitor, but I expect that we can manage..."

He chose seven pairs of shoes, a lead-loaded cane and a fly-switch, before we relaxed and became more acquainted.

Business being over, we left Aslam, and went to an outdoor café for Turkish coffee.

His name, he told me, was Emir Yakub, and I had no doubt that, even if this were not his true name, he was certainly of the Kurdish nobility. Having coffee with this hawk-faced, authoritative and cultured man was like stepping back into the thirteenth century. His conversation was interesting, and interlarded with pious phrases. Almost everything that he said had a flavor of power. I cannot be more explicit. Perhaps it was just what people call "personality."

He seemed to know Oxford well, and spoke of "The Turl" and "The Bod" as one who had probably been an undergraduate there. But when he said a phrase in English it was heavily accented. Not much could be gleaned from his talk about what his *métier* was. He knew Geneva, which might have pointed to the League of Nations or diplomatic service. Yet for one who seemed not a day over forty, he had covered a lot of ground.

The Emir did not conceal his curiosity about me. "What languages do you speak? Did you take a degree? In which countries are your relatives domiciled? What do you think of the British, the Egyptians, the Arabs? Did you join the warriors of Islam in the anti-Jewish war? Is your interest in political and military things a hobby, or have you any training or experience?"

I was feeling like a candidate for I-know-not-what when the Emir rose and said, in very rapid Persian, slurring all the words into a blur that could hardly be understood, "Honor me, please, tomorrow night, if you have no prior engagement, for dinner at eight, at the Mena House Hotel."

I bowed acceptance. "It is I who am honored, O Emir."

But he did not take his leave at once. We walked together into the street as the call to the afternoon prayer was ringing through the heat-haze, and he led me toward a small mosque, sandwiched between a bakery and a school. As we entered he whispered – ostensibly occupied with untying his shoelace – "I consign you to God's Keeping (Goodbye): he will follow me, go your own way."

It was only then that I noticed that a little, dirty, tarbooshed figure who had been standing outside the shoemaker's shop was taking off his shoes beside us...

I drove out toward the Pyramids to keep the appointment, little clearer in my mind as to the real identity of the Emir than I had been before. Nobody that I knew had heard of a Kurdish chief of that name. From my window I had watched for the surveillance that apparently haunted Yakub, but it was not being extended to me, it seemed.

As I entered the lush foyer of the Mena House, a page asked my name, and he handed me a note: "Please take Car Registration Number MSR 57854 from the hotel, and drive toward Pyramids. Ignition key in lock, Y."

I had been working very hard writing up notes and developing films. With no fixed plans for my next point of travel, I was in a sufficiently fluid frame of mind to follow this thing to the end, even if it was a joke, a trap or the offer of a job. I was not even thinking deeply about the possible implications. Most people, I believe, at one time or another, find themselves in a frame of mind in which they are not disposed to think: what they want is action. So they go out anywhere, perhaps to a dance.

Situated as I was, I looked around for signs of possible interest, saw none, tipped the Nubian boy, went outside, had got into the Buick convertible with the number-plate which the Emir Yakub had left for me.

As I started it up, the thinking process seemed suddenly to switch on. What was going on? How did he know that I could drive? And I had no Egyptian driving license. He may only want me to cat's-paw this car for him, so that his gang can steal it...

The Pyramids are no distance from Mena House, just outside Cairo. In about three minutes I saw the commanding figure of the Emir at the roadside, dressed in a Palm Beach suit, with a fez and walking stick, just in front of me.

"Salams, Emir, where are we going?"

"Forgive the inconvenience, I had some business to attend to... Go home, Anwar!"

A small boy, looking like any ordinary Egyptian peasant urchin, and cheekily grinning astride a small donkey, placed his hand on his heart in salutation, kicked the animal's sides, and trotted off. I had not even noticed him until that moment.

I thought I might be told a bit more than this.

"I am hungry, and we cannot eat pyramids, O Kurdish Emir."

Yakub was all smiles now. I had not seen him like this at our first meeting. "Come along, you Afghan wild-man, and see if you can sate yourself on what I've got for you."

He got into the driver's seat, hared back to Cairo, and headed for Heliopolis. This was real cloak-and-dagger stuff.

Yakub offered me a cigarette from a gold case, flicked on the radio, indicated the lighter on the dashboard.

I decided to use a more subtle approach. "Is there any way in which I can be of service to you? If you feel that, if I knew more – "

He cut me short. "I am a friend of Abdullah Effendi, and he says that the melon seeds that you gave him have flourished in Damascus!"

Then I knew that I could trust him. Abdullah was a very old friend of our family. Emir Yakub had added the last phrase in the immemorial way of the East to identify friends from foes. It was a random watchword, a reference to something that was known between Abdullah and myself, a trivial thing, yet it proved that Abdullah had told Yakub somehow, to identify himself.

But I still did not know anything. Abdullah was a very old friend, a landowner in Syria, who spent most of his time, as far as I could remember, upon a book which he was said to have been writing for the past twenty years...

Yakub had checked up on me, and had contacted Abdullah, and obtained this code-word, all in a matter of twenty-eight hours! That much I did know...

The Buick ate up the kilometers, and we turned into a gravel driveway of one of those immense Pasha-built villas which almost overlook Heliopolis racetrack.

We gave the car to a servant to garage, and walked a hundred yards to the *next* house, whose door was already being held open by a Nubian with a crimson robe and white sash.

The events that followed may have taken some time to see, but they more than made up for it.

We were shown into what seemed like a cupboard, whose door was then shut. After a couple of minutes in darkness, the back of the cupboard opened like a door, with the shelves and wallpaper on it, and we walked down a staircase, along a passage, then upstairs again, until I realized that we must be in yet another house.

Another door opened. Now I was in the *Arabian Nights*.

Two black Sudanese, with bared swords, gripped me by the forearms. Deferentially, with heads bowed, they walked me along a corridor into an immense room. This seemed a cross between a hall and a courtyard. I immediately recognized it – even if only from ancient miniatures – as a traditional throne-room such as was used by the Sultans of old: and this one was complete with Sultan.

Servants stood at regular intervals along the walls, one for each marble pillar. In the middle of the court there played a fountain with colored water. The odor of incense filled the air. Sitting on a large velvet cushion at the far end of the hall was the "Sultan." Ranged on either side of the fountain's oblong basin were those who could be recognized as courtiers and ministers.

Yakub came forward and freed me from the unwelcome attentions of the negroes. Together we walked slowly to where the great man sat.

As we advanced, he inclined his head.

When we were within about five yards of the enthroned figure, who wore a Persian robe and jeweled red turban, Yakub went down on one knee, and placed a small, chased and jeweled dagger at the feet of the Prince. It was the token of allegiance.

The Prince smiled, and looked at me. I was not sure what to do, so I merely looked at him. On his green robe were delicate arabesque designs, worked in golden thread. On the right breast was an ornamented version of the Imperial Cipher used by the former Caliphs and the Sultans of Turkey.

If I had not known that this was the twentieth century and that there was no Commander of the Faithful, I would have thought myself in the presence of the Caliph of All Islam, the Shadow of God on Earth, the Peacock of the World, the...

Yakub was speaking, in Persian. "...Commander of the Faithful, Shadow of Allah, Leader! This is so-and-so, son of such-and-such, Laird of such a place, of the Fatimite Family."

He looked at me. Just in time I remembered to say the traditional phrase which should end such an introduction:

"...Aspiring to be a Sacrifice for thy life if needed, come to do homage: may you live for ever!"

By now the whole thing had me in its grip. I no longer thought anything was fantastic, even unusual. Now I know what an actor means by "getting into the skin of the part." Everything was so contrived that, as far as anything was concerned, this *was* the Caliph of Islam, and I was here to salute him. Again my thought-processes were benumbed, and this time I did not even realize it.

Now the Imam spoke. "I adjure you, in the Name of Allah, not to speak or write of this meeting for six months; not to divulge at any time the location of this place." He took hold of my clothes, which is the Arab and Muslim way of inflicting a compulsory oath upon anyone. I had nothing against that.

"Willingly, O Imam, Leader."

"In Allah's name, then." He indicated a place next to him, and I sat down.

Coffee was brought, and music started to play from an alcove behind the Imam. The whole scene came sharply into my mind again some time later, when I was received in very much the same manner by King Saud, the real traditionist.

The Imam had the fairish coloring of the Arab, and the stature of a Kurd or Afghan. He must have been about fifty or perhaps a little more. On his hand there was a large green stone, set in gold, and a tiny green cord on his left breast showed that he was himself of the Fatimite Family – the descendants of Muhammad the Prophet, in whose line the supreme political and religious command of all Islam is believed by many to be vested.

He seemed a kindly man; nothing at first betrayed any glimmering of fanaticism in those large, dark eyes. His ears were small and well-shaped, hands large, with long fingers that were beautifully kept. On his feet he wore a pair of jeweled slippers.

And the story he told me was the most fantastic one that I have ever heard. I spent over four hours there on that occasion. We were regaled with fruits, sweetmeats, music and eventually a gargantuan feast in real oriental style.

With his own hands he selected some of the choicest delicacies, and pressed them upon me. When I left he gave me a copy of the Qur'an written in his own hand.

The City of Mecca, showing the Courtyard of the Great Mosque

Pilgrims in Mecca: The Sayed Ikbal Ali Shah (center) with his personal assistant and members of his family

But what he told me! The world of Islam was in ferment. There are various schools of thought about most matters. We have emerged from the period of Western domination into a state of near-anarchy where nationalism is uppermost. The fate of the peoples of Islam, from Morocco to Java, was in the hands of politicians, to a great extent, who were interested only in their own careers.

To this I had to agree. I felt the same way myself.

"The world is divided, now, into two groups, which are jockeying for power; they will clash, unless there is any reason why this should not be so. History shows us that always when there have been two Powers in the world, they have eventually clashed.

"There is, however, a Third Force: the Force of Islam! This Force can muster 400,000,000 people. It has within itself the manpower, materials and territory to be the greatest empire ever."

All this I already knew, and I knew that many people running Muslim groups, whether in Arabia or Pakistan, Egypt or China, had the same idea.

"You agree with me. So do all other thinking Muslims. But, how are we to achieve unity, for our own good, and for that of the world?"

I told the Imam that I thought that such a movement would have to come from the people, just as Islam itself had been a people's movement, and that it had been welded into the greatest empire ever, already, in former times, by people who worked for the cause, and not for themselves.

Then came the *dénouement*. "Yes, but you have left out one important factor. In life, as has been acknowledged by many, and would be recognized by many more if they would face up to it, there must be an *élite*. By an *élite* I mean that some people are more gifted than others. It is not a matter only of opportunity that all men are not equal!"

This, too, I knew to be true.

"Well, then, we must teach the people that Islam is founded on unity and equality as far as equality is possible. But there will always be leaders, and this is something that we must not forget.

"But we cannot unite Muslim countries by a stroke of the pen. We cannot compose differences by any other means than example and force; the twin bases of human life and particularly of law.

"In order to attain that power and to set that example effectively, we must bring achievements actually to bear on the people most concerned. This can be done only through the machinery of Government. It is not practicable to *initiate* this movement through the usual channels of parliamentary democracy, because the rot has set in too far.

"We all know that parliamentary democracy is a makeshift process, and that it is of limited use. It has its function, but it is not a panacea for all ills.

"Therefore we, who are the *élite*, we, who have worked for many years, we are to take the initiative!"

His eyes were really blazing now, and I felt in his every word a power such as few men have the ability to project.

"We shall take power in one of the Muslim countries. This we will do by force, though it will not involve much bloodshed. There will be a sort of a coup. We have trained men to take over important posts, whether administrative or technical, or even military.

"We will capture, at one blow, the people who matter in that country, and the rest will fall into shape. Even if we are wrong, which is unlikely, we cannot be *worse* than those already in power.

"Then we will streamline and Islamize everything. We will go back to the Qur'an and the Sayings of the Prophet. We will make ourselves strong, respected and loved. In this way we will fear nobody: and none will attack us, for we will be a threat to none.

"We shall be a benevolent dictatorship, with the *élite* always in the background. People are like children, and they have to be guided. And this Secret Power behind the throne will continue throughout the ages.

"People in other countries will emulate us. When we have set up our model state, others will follow. If they do not then we can extend to another. Every revolution will have the appearance of a national one, so there will be no intervention by outside Powers."

I really was most intrigued. Whether this man was a paranoiac did not seem to matter. At least he was honest; I could not doubt that for a moment.

Naturally, the first thing that comes to mind is that, however good a Government would be, would there be no possibility of abuse of power, intrigue and so forth? I asked this question.

"My friend, you have spoken well. Yes, there are these dangers, and a thousand others as well. But the thing has gone too far for mere palliatives. We must take the risk. I am prepared to answer to God, and all of us should be so prepared."

For the rest of what he told me, I must wait until the time limit expires. For he imposed upon me a further period of silence covering the more immediate intentions of the movement. But I am convinced that this man, and his followers, will exert a powerful effect upon the entire life of the Middle East, and even beyond.

During this meeting, and the two subsequent ones at which the Imam received me, he said several times, "I am making amends for Hasan, son of Sabah, of our clan."

This was one of the clues to the identity of the man.

For, many centuries ago, in Persia there arose an Imam, who promised his followers Paradise if they died in his service. He was known as the Great Assassin, and it is from the name of these people that the English word itself is derived (see any etymological dictionary).

Hasan, son of Sabah, became the leader of a group called the Ismailis, dedicated himself to the aim of becoming Master of the World, and settled in the impregnable castle of Alamut. The story is familiar to Easterners, but perhaps less well known in the West.

Hasan himself had been the disciple of a man preaching very similar views to those of the Imam whom I was meeting. He had created a synthetic "paradise" in a luxuriant valley, where his followers were taken, drugged and allowed to awake. When they found themselves there, it seemed like nothing less than Heaven. There were fountains and gardens, rich fruits and maidens to minister to their every want.

Then, having been again drugged with hashish, the *Hashishin* (Assassins) were taken away, and told that they would be able to reenter Paradise only upon death: and at that, only if they died obeying the direct orders of Hasan, son of Sabah, of the Family of Hashim, the Fatimite.

Their bid for world hegemony was frustrated only by one element which they had not taken into account: the frightful irruption of the all-conquering Mongols into the Middle East. Halaku the Destroyer wiped them out.

But before this happened, more than half the thrones of Asia had been rocked by the mysterious assassinations of the Hashishin. The King of Bokhara was stabbed, Emperor Saladin attacked, even the Crusaders were harried by these fearless fanatics sent out by Hasan, the "Old Man of the Mountains," as he was called by some.

This is what can happen with a plan of the kind revealed to me by the new and anonymous Imam. Both ideas came from the same root, probably certain mystical schools which flourished during that time. Strangely enough, Hasan was a schoolfellow of Omar Khayyam, the Poet Laureate of Persia. Those who can prove descent from Muhammad are said by many to be the heirs to the leadership of Islam; and though the Prophet himself stated that there was no nobility in blood so important as piety, yet tradition dies hard, and several dynasties with greater or lesser pretensions to descent from him have ruled ever since, in localized areas. Among these families, too, are some which are not now possessed of any actual territorial power (such as Sultan Muhammad Shah – the Aga Khan). Then there are the *de facto* kings, like the Hashimites of Iraq and Jordan, and King Idris of Libya.

But Arabia itself, my present goal, was ruled by Abdul-Aziz, son of Saud, and it was under the patronage of the Wahabis rather than the Hashimites that I was to revisit the kingdom of my forefathers.

There is a saying that "everything has a minimum time" – often quoted as an Eastern excuse for inaction. Yet my Cairo sojourn proved to my satisfaction that, active or inactive, there was a further wait before the time when I could set off for the Holy City of Islam.

CHAPTER VI

Marching Orders

I WALKED FROM Azhar University, far away in the Old City, through the teeming, broiling streets of Cairo toward the capital's "West End." If words like melting-pot and kaleidoscope hummed through my brain, it was only because they fitted the scene better than anything else I could think of. Impressions crowded into the mind so fast that they seemed to blur one another until either the heat or the multiplicity of activities dazed me.

I had been in Cairo three months. I had a fair knowledge of the language: and I could understand, as a Muslim who had lived for years in the West, most of the things that were going on. But I could not get used to them going together like this. It was as if a giant anthill had been invaded by bits and pieces from another kind of life – and the ants were doing all they could to absorb this Western culture, with varying degrees of success.

From every café of the *Musky* twentieth-century loudspeakers blared passages from the seventh-century Qur'an. In one corner of the huge *suk* a tinsmith was hammering a Coca-Cola advertisement into rims for an ox-cart wheel. Outside the thousand-year-old Azhar University, with its air-conditioning and antique carpets, stood a long row of dollar-grinning American cars.

Even the people in the streets seemed a little thrown out of balance by the impact of Westernism, in spite of the fact that they had known it for centuries. This was shown to quite a remarkable extent by the assorted clothing of the populace. The standard turnout of the workers seemed to be a complete ex-British Army khaki drill uniform, with sandals and a skullcap. The Armenian, Greek and Coptic shopkeepers seemed to prefer to orientalize themselves, and to adopt Arabic names. The swarthy Sudanese from the deep south, complete with fantastic scarrings denoting tribal affiliation, were either immaculately robed in ultra-Arab style or else wearing the latest American-style clothes.

This was the East and West. In addition everywhere was to be seen the profound impact of the rediscovery of ancient Egypt. In spite of the Islamic strictness against Pharaonic ways, one saw names, pictures and even houses which were based upon the culture of ancient dynastic times.

As I emerged into the more modern part of the town, with its skyscrapers and neon signs, its donkey-carts and Cadillacs, its beggars and millionaire cotton men, a crowd watched a group of young men standing at a busy traffic intersection. A number of stunted, unhappy-looking policemen with staves edged forward apprehensively.

I stopped to listen to the shouting of the youths: "*Allaho-Akbar, Allaho-Akbar, Allaho-Akbar! Subhanullah Wahda!*"

My neighbor shrugged and indicated the police. "They dare not touch them, even though they are outlawed members of the Muslim Brotherhood. They are reciting prayers!"

I moved away as the Brothers continued to demonstrate their presence as a unit: "God is Greatest! God is Greatest! God is Greatest! Praise be to God, the *Undivided!*"

As I emerged into Sharia Ibrahim Pasha, the streets suddenly seemed to fill with troops. Looking upward I saw machine-guns being posted on the tops of the buildings. I took out my camera, and set the exposure dial. It was wrenched out of my hand.

The police captain asked to see my passport. "Stand here. I will give you your camera back in a few minutes."

"What is wrong? I am a friend of Egypt, on my way to Mecca. I don't want to photograph anything secret: but what is going on?"

"I cannot tell you. In any case you cannot move for the next half-hour. All traffic must come to a standstill. If you wait here you will see something interesting."

More and more troops. They formed up in two lines, facing one another on each side of the avenue. Crowds began to collect, and were marshaled by the police. A radio van crawled through the silenced street, broadcasting the national anthem.

After about an hour's wait in that burning heat, pressed against unhygienic bodies, with another bunch of Brethren chanting "No man is better than another man in the sight of God save him who is more pious" – a saying of the Prophet Muhammad – I realized that King Farouk was about to pass this way.

The man standing next but one to me was marched off under arrest for calling Farouk a "son of a camel." He was screaming and begging for mercy. Nobody seemed particularly enthusiastic about the Sovereign, but most were a little more discreet.

Then Klaxon horns sounded, one after another, far away down the street. Something was approaching. The police and troops stood to attention. Machine-guns on rooftops were trained on the crowd. As the hooters came nearer and nearer I caught a glimpse of a blood-red streamlined car, with a fat bespectacled figure in the back, and all windows closed, shooting past. I tapped the captain on the arm. "Give me my camera, and let me go, please, Colonel."

"Sorry, you must wait." Nobody had stirred. I waited.

Another series of Klaxons, another identical blood-red car, another hunched figure in the back. This happened five times, at intervals of about three minutes. One of them must have been Farouk, but which? They all had the same number-plate. The "Son of a String of Pearls" must have been reading about the fabulous Haroun-el-Rashid, who slept in a different bed every night.

The Muslim Brothers behind me were chanting: "The *Muslims* are one hand, like unto the bricks in a wall. All are important, but none is more important than the other!" I got my camera back, and carried on my weary way.

A crowded tram, carrying so many people that its very outlines seemed obscured, came clanging toward me. I got a shot of it as it passed. By now I was not in a very good temper; so when the camera was snatched out of my hand by a zoot-suited youth wearing sunglasses, I grabbed his spectacles and ground them underfoot.

"Son of a dog! Accursed thief! Give me my camera, and I may decide not to crush thee like a worm!"

Immediately he calmed down. "I am a student. You are a foreigner. I do not like to see things which are shameful to our country being photographed. Forgive me, don't hurt me!"

Unfortunately I come from rather easily inflamed Afghan stock, so I berated him thoroughly for about three minutes.

I told him that I could not see any shame in having overcrowded trams. That I didn't like the look of his face. That I hoped that he was as active in doing something constructive for his country as he was in annoying foreigners. In any case it was not his country any more than mine. I was a Muslim, and Muslim lands belonged to the Muslims, equally. This always has effect, because it is an argument based upon the Pan-Islamic concept of Islam and the sayings of Muhammad. He slunk away. Under other circumstances I might have made a friend of him. I made a mental note to try conciliation before aggression in future.

I mention this instance because it is typical of many such happenings that I experienced almost daily in Egypt. There is an immense amount of vitality in the younger Egyptians. But they do not seem to know where, if anywhere, they are going. For this reason they are very divided among themselves, and united only by the fact that the majority are members of the Muslim faith. They are often most sincere, many are extremely likeable. But they derive their experience of life and politics second-hand from those "clever" books, full of ingenious arguments, which are written by tongue-in-the-cheek politicians, or translated from English and French. These are typical questions that I was asked at a meeting of Egyptian students which I addressed:

1. What is foam? It says in the holy writings that something ephemeral is like unto foam: it gathers upon water and has being, yet it disappears and has no further existence. What, then, is it?
2. Would you advise me to stay in Egypt and look after my family, or journey to Europe and seek military training, to prepare myself for the struggle against the unbelievers?
3. How can we train the West in Islamic civilization?
4. Do you not believe that unity in the Middle East can only be achieved when one country makes a start? How can one country start this campaign for unity with all the others, and will it not be necessary to extirpate all existing vested interests before we can go ahead?

I kept a note of these questions as a sort of miniature cross-section of thought among young students, because this was the type of query that continually cropped up.

All these thoughts were in my mind as I arrived at the hotel where the Saudi-Arabian Delegation to the Arab League's

Session was entrenched. As I entered the immense and luxury-filled foyer, I tried to readjust my thoughts to Mecca and the problem of getting there, taking pictures and getting out after performing the Pilgrimage.

The main lounge was a brilliant scene, reminiscent of great diplomatic occasions in pre-war Europe. Attachés, members of the Arab Legion, immaculate secretaries and delegates, sat with their ladies or in apparent conference at the flower-decked tables.

I knew that Prince Faisal, the Minister of Foreign Affairs of Saudi Arabia, was there, and made my way boldly up to the frock-coated head porter. "Please send my card up to His Royal Highness of Saudi Arabia."

I took a seat, and wondered whether the proud Wahabi would see me. Something which complicated my visit to the Arabian Peninsula was the fact that my family was reputed not to be too popular there. In the first place a (totally incorrect) rumor had it that my father had been on the side of certain Indian troublemakers who had challenged King ibn Saud in the 1920s. In actual fact he had used every weapon in his power to overcome them, and had eventually succeeded.

More important, perhaps, was the fact that we trace our direct descent from the Caliph Musa-Kazim, of the Prophet's family. And this family – the Hashimites – were not popular with the Wahabi Arabians because it was thought that some of them might claim suzerainty of Arabia as their historical right. King Abdullah of Jordan was thus a kinsman of ours, and a close friend. It was stated that he and the aging King ibn Saud were enemies. Saudis said that this was because the Hashimites were friends of the British puppets, even. Hashimites claimed the estrangement to be due to the fact that the Saudis had displaced the lawful Hashimite ruler of the Hejaz.

For this reason I had been warned not to style myself by my title, which betrayed my descent from Muhammad. But I remembered that Prince Faisal and his father Saud knew my father, and hoped for the best. In any case, it would not be too easy to refuse anyone access to the Holy City, if he were a bona fide Muslim on a pilgrimage.

Five or ten minutes had passed. A tall figure dressed in Arabian robes hovered at my elbow. "Sayed Edris? Please follow me."

As soon as we got out of the lift I was almost pushed through a guarded door. Inside the room, drawn up in the traditional circle of chairs which is the court of an Emir, were the Saudi Delegation. I made my way to the center of the group, to the commanding figure of Emir Faisal, in his royal headdress of gold-thread circlets and white summer robe.

As I approached he rose and smiled. People have said that he is a stern man, with a very high idea of the niceties of Arab social procedure. I saw him as the very archetype of an aristocratic Arab. Tall, slim, hawk-nosed and proud, he had that strange magnetism which I was to see again in his father, the warrior King ibn Saud, who had conquered the entire land of Arabia for the Wahabite dynasty. He looked surprisingly young: younger than he had seemed when I met him as a child, twenty years before.

On either side, respectfully silent, were the Ambassador in Cairo, the Ambassador from London, and other celebrities.

I kissed Faisal's hand. At this moment there was nearly a contretemps. I had forgotten that my camera was slung in its leather case under my armpit. As I bent forward it slipped and swung down, very much like a shoulder holster for something more dangerous. There was a distinct gasp from some of the company. But Faisal is a man of iron nerve. He merely smiled, and asked me how I was.

As I sat beside him, he asked me the reasons for my coming thus far, where I proposed to go afterward, and questions of this kind.

I told him that I was a pilgrim, that I proposed to visit the Holy City, and that I would very much welcome the opportunity of presenting my respects to his distinguished father, who knew my own father.

He turned to the Saudi Ambassador in Cairo. "The Sayed is our guest. You will be able to make all the arrangements, O Sheikh?"

The Ambassador bowed. I thanked the Emir, and withdrew.

I was on my way to Saudi Arabia. The following day I had my passport visaed and inscribed by the Saudi-Arabian Embassy: "By Order of the Emir Faisal, Foreign Minister of Saudi Arabia, Viceroy of the Hejaz..."

Hospitality among the Arabs is fabled for its magnificence. It was good to see that the Wahabis, stern puritans though they are, were true inheritors of that wonderful tradition.

I had only to book my passage.

CHAPTER VII

Red Sea Journey

Ours was not a pilgrim ship – not, at any rate, at first. Suez seemed as Suez so often is: hot and dusty, built on a kind of slope, as punishing to the feet as the taximen's demands are to the purse.

Stamped deeply in its shops as well as by its street signs with the unmistakable presence of the British Army, it felt somehow uneasy, brooding.

I was now a pilgrim, heading southward through the Canal and the Red Sea, bound for Jeddah, the pilgrim port of Saudi Arabia.

When he saw my visa, the passport officer shrugged to his colleague of the Customs. *Hujjaj*,[1] it seemed from his remarks, never had anything much dutiable: "*Andu mafish haga!*"[2]

I wondered, as I always do, why there should be so much preoccupation about people leaving the country. I had paid – quite generously, I thought – for the privilege of having my baggage examined upon entering. But there it was, and the usual procedure would have to be followed.

It is difficult to say whether this ritual is naive, kindly or even lax. But the fact that I had seen about twenty of my

---

[1]   *Hujjaj* = Pilgrims.
[2]   "He hasn't got anything."

future traveling companions go through it meant that I was prepared.

Thus, when the Customs man fixed me with a penetrating gaze, I was not surprised to hear the exultant *Haa-Haa!* of his fellow, strategically stationed directly behind me – and calculated, it seemed, to cause the intending smuggler immediately to leap out of his skin with fear and confess all.

Having survived this, I walked up the gangplank into a smallish vessel, clean enough but somehow too all-metal for this broiling sun. When we got under way, I was to think of this, to reflect that if I felt discomfort at the unyielding character of a steel ship, how much more aching must have been the regret of those used to the generous movement of wooden walls, with the white canvas billowing out above.

Both the captain and the inevitably red-haired engineer were Scots; most of the crew hailed from the Valley of the Nile. The passengers seemed to be of every nation except Egypt.

As we started, the call to midday prayer sounded from the third class and steerage, where the patient pilgrims sat. A Turkoman in felt boots (he had walked almost all the way from Persia) stood leading the worshippers facing Meccaward. Only three, so far, were dressed in pilgrim white: Ahmed the Somali, his wife, and their six-year-old son Abdullah. On our own deck the Saudi Sheikh, the Syrian agronomist and two Turkish journalists had already made friends. An American, bound for Aden, read Sherlock Holmes and called for tea every half-hour. The incessant blurred rhythm of Arabic music haunted every corner of the deck; loudspeakers carried the Cairo radio programs from dawn to dusk.

As we negotiated the chain of connected lakes which make up the Canal, two days" steaming brought about a complete change of mood aboard the ship. It was as if we were in another world: everything of Cairo had been forgotten.

There were no smells, no teeming hordes of curious and idle lingerers, nothing but the throb of the engines and the white birds circling overhead. We were but four days from Jeddah now, from the land to see which some of us had walked for years, others, saved all their lives.

The first unusual event was the complete abandoning of all distinctions between first- and third-class passengers. Though they spent most of their time in their own part of the ship, all passengers mixed freely and made one another welcome. One, more pious, perhaps, than others, prevailed upon the radio officer to disconnect the relaying of music. Under awnings the faithful sat, prayed or read books.

The Westernized first-class travelers now paced the deck in flowing robes: the Syrian still watered his plants five times a day, and he was growing a beard. I, too, stopped shaving, because it would have been discourteous to appear before the King clean-shaven – if I was to see the King, that was.

The American complained that the puritanical Saudi Sheikh had thrown all playing cards overboard as "inventions of the Devil." One might almost have said – if this were not a phrase with completely irrelevant associations – that we were reverting to type. This was the transition period. The women passengers formed a group of their own, under the presidency of the wife of one of the clerics of the Mecca Sanctuary, who was returning from a visit to her sister in Cairo. She coached them in the recitations and prayers to be used during the Pilgrimage, and spoke of the work that she was doing in social welfare and for the benefit of children in the Hejaz.

I seemed to be the person with the best grasp of English, and the American attached himself to me. He questioned me rather narrowly as to the motives for my journey, what I expected to get out of it, and the conditions of life in Saudi Arabia. Even in his case I maintained my policy of secrecy about the intention to photograph the Shrine – just in case. There are a lot of Americans employed by the Saudi Government in the less-restricted parts of the country.

Eventually the American asked me to take him to Mecca. He would be allowed, he said, to land at Jeddah. This was not a forbidden city. Once there, it would be possible, though not easy, to get into Mecca. He was willing to pay all expenses. He was willing, even, to reimburse me for my trouble. But I had troubles enough, and I told him that I would like to do it, but that being on the Pilgrimage I could not be a party to such a deception. Was he a Muslim? He was not. "In that case you would not get much benefit out of going to Mecca."

But he wanted to be the first American to go there. After all, Mecca was far more impenetrable than Tibet. He knew, he'd been to Tibet. "Nothing to it," he told me.

If he became a Muslim would he be able to get in? I told him it was possible, but it would take time and perseverance. It might take years before he were sufficiently trusted. Even then, a false move could mean death. It has happened before. I reminded him that times were even more difficult than when such men as Burton got through in disguise. Today you have to run the gauntlet of walkie-talkie apparatus, identity cards and pilgrim passports – plus having to know the rituals and ways of Islam.

Suspense, suppressed excitement, the feeling of a profound experience soon to come, throbbed in every pilgrim heart as we neared Jeddah. Then, in the brilliant hardness of the early morning sunlight, Saudi Arabia was sighted.

For the first time, as the white-robed faithful lined the rails, I heard the immemorial pilgrim chant, that was to be repeated a thousand times during my stay there: *Labbayk, Allahumma, Labbayk!* ("We are here, O Lord, we are here!")

Gleaming whitely, coral-built beyond those treacherous reefs through which ships cannot pass to her quaysides,

Sign on the road to Mecca

Public letter-writer, Mecca

Jeddah beckoned, and Mecca: only fifty miles eastward through the desert.

Amid the cheers of the crew and chanting of the first chapter of the Qur'an, we got into small boats and were ferried to the jetties where annually upward of a hundred thousand Muslims land, from Morocco, Java, and almost every Eastern land.

Even before we reached the shore, striking evidence of the contrasts in a changing East abounded. Perched within the harbor on coral outcrops, fishermen were angling for the food which makes up so much of the diet of Jeddah's poorer citizens.

Large hoardings, inscribed in Arabic, Indonesian and half a dozen other tongues, proclaimed: *Pilgrims, Saudi Arabia Welcomes You.* Bronzed and hefty porters, their girdled costumes unchanged since Abraham's day, unloaded a Pakistani ship to the strains of the traditional, haunting shanty of their trade. Stacked in immense heaps, merchandise from all the world lay awaiting Customs examination in the huge concrete buildings so new that the roofs were actually being put on while they were in active use. This was just a symptom of the age of plenty which multi-million American oil royalties have brought to Arabia today.

The Turkoman was already in tears as we landed, and spoke of the sand getting in his eyes as we shook hands in farewell.

Before Ibn Saud conquered this country, the peninsula was divided into the austere northern part – Nejd – and this, the southern, easygoing Hejaz. Even today, thirty years later, the King keeps his capital in Riyadh – toward the Persian Gulf – and foreign embassies accredited to Saudi Arabia must remain in Jeddah, dotted in their graceful mansions around the curving inland bay.

Each group of pilgrims went to the arched Hall of Pilgrim Reception, for refreshment, identification, and allocation of guides. I put my bags on the Customs bench, and opened them.

My camera was slung around my neck – looking very much like one of those leather Qur'an cases which many religious people carry.

I had not expected any special treatment. But as soon as I presented my passport, a gorgeously robed sheikh of the Administration of Hospitality took charge of me. I was ushered into a modern American car, and driven rapidly through the dazzling ultra-modern streets to the *Diafa*, guest-apartments of the King.

Entering the thickly carpeted, cool vastness of the hall of reception, I felt some diffidence in giving my name to the manager. This white-robed figure, with the twin camel-hair circlets of the bedouin on his head, I felt, might harbor some antagonism toward descendants of the Prophet, on political grounds. I knew that Ibn Saud would not permit any privileged class, and expected some sort of reaction. However this may once have been, it is no longer the case.

I was announced to the assembled gathering with many a high-flown title. Grave, bearded faces courteously composed, they rose, and we kissed each other's hands.

When I got to the middle of the horseshoe of armchairs, a giant, red-bearded elder noticed my hesitation. "I am the doctor in charge of the Quarantine," he told me, with an Edinburgh lilt to his excellent Arabic. Like all foreigners in Saudi Arabia he wore the white robe and brown bedouin cloak woven from the hair of the Kuwait camel.

I was later to meet several such men: engineers, doctors, scientists, from Britain, America, Czechoslovakia or France: Saudi officials now, and remarkably confident in their adopted characters of what are locally called *Musta"*
Arabin – "Arabized ones" – just as Robert of Chester and

Michael Scot were known as Musta" Arabi in the Moorish Spain of an earlier age.

Upon reflection, it is hard to say why one should at first feel this change to be so odd. Why should it be taken for granted that an Arab may live in Britain as the British do, yet the reverse appear so unusual or difficult?

I sent a telegram by radio to the King at Riyadh, announcing my arrival, and stating that I was ready to fly to the capital to render him homage, after performing my essential Pilgrimage duties in the Holy City.

The new Post Office building where I sent this message was an eye-opener. Today's Arab buildings in Jeddah are built in a blending of the ancient and Western styles, and equipped with what seems a complete disregard for expense. Faisal Street (named after the Viceroy of the Hejaz) runs through the center of the new town, right up to the docks. And this, at the other end of the city, joins the Pilgrim Way, the newly macadamed road leading to Mecca itself.

Dominated on both sides by immense steel and concrete structures – apartment-houses, banks and administrative buildings – fish-tailed Cadillacs purr through its sweeping length. You will not find many places like Jeddah in the Middle East. Yet, in spite of an almost bewildering array of Western products and machines, Jeddah still holds much of that indefinable quality which we cannot analyze, and even today must call the magic of the East.

Dressed in my one-piece, unstitched robe of cotton, with sandaled feet, with bare head in a temperature of 113 degrees, I wandered farther afield. This is the obligatory garb of all who come to make the Pilgrimage. None must wear silk or anything that would show social distinctions.

The town's cosmopolitan cafés, although they serve Western soft drinks as well as the harsh Nejdi coffee, do not cater for any superficially Westernized clientele. Although the fierce-eyed, armed-to-the-teeth bedouin from the desert does stand out in contrast with his more sophisticated urban compatriot, yet, for all this, both the well-trained Arab radio engineer or oil technician, and the tribesman from the wilds, continue to conform to age-old tradition: the code which increasing prosperity only seems to make more binding. This is probably because the Royal Family set the fashion.

This historic headcloth, bound with interlinked ropes, and a voluminous camelhair cloak, remain their common heritage. The advent of newspapers and the radio, indeed, actually appear to have increased the Arab's innate appreciation of his own way of life. This is one of the most striking things about Saudi Arabia today. Unlike so many Eastern lands, the Saudi really feel that they are on a basis of equality with everyone else.

Ever since the Turks were driven out of the country, during the First World War, Arabians have distrusted foreigners and their ways. For this reason King Abdul-Aziz ibn Saud had to combat a very natural reluctance on the part of the more conservative elements to welcome people and machines which they did not fully understand.

On the other hand, the real nomad of the desert has always been free. Secure in the wilderness of the sands, following desert tracks known only to himself, he has completely escaped that fear of the unknown which haunted settled townsmen. It is from the ranks of the bedouin, therefore, that come the country's new doctors, air pilots and mechanics.

Beyond the British Embassy lie the many-storied mansions of the merchant princes, their delicately carved rosewood lattices ajar to capture any fugitive breeze. Evidence of the invigorating role of oil royalties rises on every side, everywhere. Hawk-eyed bedouin chiefs drive cars of such modernity that I had not seen their like even in Cairo or Beirut. Here East meets West, one feels, and the two mingle. Flowing robes may be made of nylon. Ultra-modern automobiles are upholstered in priceless antique carpeting.

Running from east to west and north to south, and still triumphantly holding its own, stretches the great collection of open-fronted shops, representing innumerable trades, which is known as the *suk*: the market which tradition says was there when King Solomon's ships called here on their voyages to the land of Punt: and where the Queen of Sheba's caravans once halted, bringing the ivory of Africa to trade for the perfumes of far Asia.

This market is truly oriental – a haphazard, winding, eminently colorful avenue of old-style commerce. It may strike a Western eye as primitive in some ways. Yet you may purchase here not only the finest products of Birmingham and Detroit, but also priceless Eastern wares. I am convinced that there is almost nothing that you cannot buy, examine or order from the world's workshops through the picturesque Jeddah *Suk*.

I bought a few things, made friends with some of the multilingual shopkeepers, yarned with them and drank innumerable cups of tea without milk, or coffee flavored with cardamoms.

As one intent upon Mecca pictures, however, with my Pilgrimage almost upon me, I had to obtain certain data for that vital occasion.

I took light readings of the shadows and sunlight at various times of the day; estimated the type of lens that I would need for the job; and thought out different ways to conceal the camera.

The technical problems were considerable. How to process the films in that heat without ice? How to conceal the camera, and yet be able to sight it? How to overcome the snag that the built-in motor of the apparatus made a terrible click when a picture was taken? If I did not, for instance, develop the films there, how would I know whether I had got suitable results? I took a number of furtive pictures in Jeddah, and developed them in my bathroom at the *Diafa*. The heat was so tremendous that the emulsion cracked and stripped off in the form of jelly.

I went to a chemist and asked for formalin or alum, to harden the film, but he told me that I would have to have a doctor's prescription: "Both are dangerous poisons!"

There was a photographer's shop in Jeddah, but I did not like to spend too much time there, because pilgrims should not be interesting themselves in cameras. They might have processed the films for me when I got back, but that would mean that the secret would be out. Eventually I ordered ice, and used this. The rumor got round that I was a secret drinker: for alcohol is utterly forbidden in Saudi Arabia, as being against the Islamic faith. In the end I decided to make my pilgrimage to the Shrine, and then come back later to take photographs, after examining the possibilities of light and the extent of surveillance exercised.

This meant that I was now to confine myself to the duties of the Pilgrimage, and nothing else.

On the Jeddah–Mecca highway, some three kilometers out of Jeddah, you will see by the side of the road a massive, futuristic palace. During the day, flags of variegated hue stream from a sort of mast mounted upon the topmost turret. By night there is an incessant, restless winking of signal lights. If you have hired a car, truck, station wagon, your driver will mutter as he passes this place: "Long live Ba-Khashab Pasha, and all his children!" – almost as if it were in invocation. He will stop for a hurried conversation with a very business-like Arab at a window in the palace wall. Coming home that night, as the twinkling lights come into sight, he will dip his headlights in salute. Day or night, Ba-Khashab Pasha's organization is exchanging signals with his fleet of cars.

Once Ba-Khashab was a humble, ordinary man, somewhere on the Saudi coastline, trying to earn a living by hiring out camels. Today, with the enormous expansion of transportation and the demand for vehicles of every kind, the Pasha (nobody knows where he got his title, since it is not a Saudi one) has worked his way up until he can loll in luxury – if he were not such a worker. He is small, middle-aged, lithe, laughing and likeable, and when I went to see him he refused to let me take his photograph, but asked what prospects there were of getting his boy into Eton or Oxford.

His case could be multiplied more than a hundredfold, throughout almost the length and breadth of Arabia. A new class of Arabs has grown up: the contractor, large farmer, industrialist. Some of the sheikhs and older aristocracy, it is true, have also benefited by the new prosperity. But the two groups never mix, though each has a vital function in the Arabia of today. "Go north, to the American oilfields of Dhaharan, if you want to see action," said Ba-Khashab. "Those Americans certainly are workers. And why are they successful? Because they have unknowingly applied the principles of Islam, of the Prophet, who said: 'I regard myself as a worker!'"

An American to whom I spoke shortly afterward gave me his version of the question. "John Q. Arab certainly is learning fast. He sure is a worker. The American way of life has gone right in there, deep."

So you can take your pick. The truth lies somewhere in the middle. The Arab does not like work without knowing that it will be rewarded. And it must be rewarded, if at all possible, by something really worthwhile. He is, in a sense, a natural capitalist.

When the Americans came into the Saudi field, they offered not only substantial royalties in advance of the sinking of even the first well: they supplied a clear hope that not only would the Government benefit by a percentage of all oil extracted, but that there would be employment and scope for local enterprise. So the Arabs and Americans could do business.

The Americans were – and still are – extremely sensitive about their position in Saudi Arabia. Every one of the 12,000 foreign employees of the Arabian-American Company is schooled and drilled and dinned with the principles of the Islamic faith and the subtleties of Arabian custom. No American would think today of venturing anywhere except where the oil company has a right to be. And even then he lives in his robes, his headcloth and rope fillets, like an Arab desert-bred.

The Americans are in on a good thing. From Dhaharan and the surrounding deserts a million barrels of petroleum are extracted *daily.* Arabian-American is sitting, as it was put to me, "right on top of the greatest oilfield in the world."

To have established this bridgehead in the sternly Wahabite – and therefore anti-Christian – part of Arabia must be counted as one of the major victories of Western business. It may be said to have been a hard-won victory, from the standpoint of pure capitalism: though I am not suggesting that the Americans feel that they have had to give too much. What I can say is that Aramco is an organization in which the winning of the oil from the sands has resulted in a sharing of advantages between Arabs and Americans alike. The Americans have built the great Mosque which is the dominating feature of the Saudi oil camp. They have drilled deep water-wells in hundreds of places, to provide vital sustenance for camels and people. They have their own technical training program for Saudis, hospitals, clinics, shops, agricultural missions, and the rest. While a large number of foreign employees are used in Dhaharan, nobody suggests that any foreigner be recruited if there is a Saudi who can do the job. Local contractors have even been set up in business by the Company, and then patronized by Aramco.

While much of the enterprise which has resulted in a new prosperity for the Saudi peninsula is directly attributable to the American spirit and sheer dogged determination, yet the gigantic personality of Abdul-Aziz ibn El-Saud can conclusively be said to have been the power behind almost everything that has been accomplished during the past twenty years.

In order to understand this fully, it will be necessary to make a very brief reference to the position of Arabia in a changing world.

According to Arab tradition, mankind's first home was somewhere in the Peninsula. Some point to Aden as the site of the Garden of Eden, others to Eve's reputed grave not far out of Jeddah. It is also believed that the Mecca Kaaba was first built by Adam himself, on the model of a house of worship in Paradise, where the angels endlessly circumambulated, praising their Lord.

Further, the Arabs of today claim descent from Abraham, through Ishmael who, they hold, was the son offered by the patriarch to God. Abraham rebuilt the Kaaba and sacred shrine of Arabia, in token of repentance for having cast Hagar out into the wilderness. Hence the sanctity of Hagar's Well in the Sanctuary – the Zam-Zam – believed to be the same stream which God caused to spring miraculously for Hagar's succor. It is, of course, known that the Arabs and Jews are both of Semitic origin, and that their languages are derived from a similar root. Hence there is some likelihood on the face of it that in pre-recorded times the Arabs followed the Hebrew religious dispensation.

While the Jews, however, maintained to a greater or lesser degree their monotheism, the Arabs, in the tribal wandering throughout the great deserts, lapsed into a theology which was based upon a number of gods. These took two forms: the main deities represented the Sun, Moon and planets, while the lesser ones were totems which watched over individual tribes.

The sanctity of Mecca remained in their observances, and the Sanctuary (*Haram*) became the home of over 300 idols. The rites of pilgrimage, adapted to the worship of the gods, continued uninterruptedly.

This was the period of the Jahiliyya ("Days of Ignorance") which existed until the seventh century of the Christian Era, when Muhammad preached a return to monotheism.

Muhammad was, as is fairly well known, a member of the most noble clan of the Arabs, the Quraish, who were shrine-keepers at the *Haram*. It was in Mecca that the first chapters of the Qur'an (literally "The Recitation") were revealed to Muhammad, as Muslims believe, by the Archangel Gabriel.

According to this mandate, Muhammad was commanded by God to lead the people out of ignorance, to make them worship one God alone, and to follow the code of morality and law which, Islam says, has been carried out through successive prophets. Islam, which means "submission to the will of God," is therefore not a new religion. According to the Qur'an it is the modern manifestation of the preaching of such people as Moses and Jesus. Islam therefore recognizes the Jewish dispensation, as does Christianity, but accepts Jesus, whom the Jews do not, on the restricted basis of his being a divinely inspired *man*, and not a divine being.

All this has definite bearing upon Arabian and world history subsequent to Muhammad's mission.

After the persecutions and trials common to all great religious teachers, Muhammad found that his preaching had eventually converted almost all Arabia. But Islam was for the whole world: this is a fundamental. So it must be spread. When he died, Muhammad had just completed his exchange of letters with neighboring rulers, calling upon them to accept Islam.

Under Muhammad's immediate successors, the Arab tribes – unified for the first time in history – poured forth from the deserts, and conquered all North Africa to the Atlantic, all the Holy Roman Empire, and what is now Turkey, Persia and Afghanistan. Under successive dynasties, Islam became the most powerful force on earth. Muslims reached the borders of France and Austria, pushed far into China, overcame all India, marched into the Russian steppes. For several hundred years the Islamic centers of learning retrieved and developed lost sciences and became the magnet for seekers after knowledge everywhere. Islam had by now become a composite civilization, as well as a religion and social order. With the entry of the Persian, Indian and European elements, a synthesis had been produced.

Then came the destruction of the military and cultural force of the new world-state. The irruption of the pagan Mongol hordes from Central Asia literally ground the Muslims into a mire of their own blood and the ruins of their cities, farms, universities. From this blow Islam has never really recovered. True, the Mongols eventually accepted Islam, but so much had been lost that it has taken nearly a thousand years to revive.

Saudi Arabia became subject to Ottoman Turkey. Deep in their desert strongholds, the bedouin were little affected by what went on in the world. But they nursed their heritage: the possession of the Qur'an, and the knowledge that it had been under Arabs and Muslims that their power had extended from Spain to China.

The Turks were driven out of Arabia by an alliance between bedouins, Hijazi Arabs and the British, in which rebellion the late T. E. Lawrence played such a part.

But the northern area, home of the Wahabites, had never really been under effective Turkish control. Even before the First World War, the Saudis – the family of Ibn Saud – were working and fighting to regain control of Nejd, their former homeland.

By 1902 the twenty-year-old Abdul-Aziz ibn El-Saud had captured the northern fortress of Riyadh. The descendants of the Prophet who were nominal rulers of Mecca in the south, and who cooperated with the British to throw off the Turkish yoke, had to leave, and set up their own small kingdoms in Iraq and Transjordan. Saud made himself master of all Peninsular Arabia.

The first period of his reorganization of the country pacified the tribes under the banner of Saud the Great. Then the "effete" south was visited with severe punishment, and all "extravagances" were put down. Domes and minarets were leveled, for example, as being importations foreign to the simple spirit of Islam.

But Ibn Saud could not go any further with his big plans for the development and uplift of the seven million Arabs without more money than any Arab could conceive of at that time. For nearly twenty years Saudi Arabia depended solely upon customs dues and the few million pounds that the pilgrims brought each year for their expenses.

Then, in 1933, King Abdul-Aziz arranged with American companies to drill for oil. I was told by one veteran of those days that the geologists were convinced that somewhere here, in the wild and hostile Wahabi country, lay the world's largest deposit. But it took them five years of wildcat (random) drilling to locate it. After they did, Saudi Arabia never had to look back.

Arabia had become front-page news. In the days just before the Second World War Germans, Italians and even the Japanese fought for oil and commercial concessions. Britain and America were reported to be at loggerheads because, it was said, Britain thought that she should have had a greater interest in the oil. Ibn Saud weathered it all. During the last war he was one of the few neutral statesmen who consistently supported the Allied cause.

When Vichy held Syria in an uneasy pro-Axis grip, and Rashid Ali el-Gailani revolted in Iraq, all seemed lost to the United Nations. Ibn Saud, as I was told in Riyadh, could easily have thrown in his lot with the Germans, and would have had little to lose. Deprived of his oil, the British and American fleets and mercantile marine would have been crippled in this part of the world. The Japanese could have made liaison with the Germans via the Arabian coastline, and the route between India and Europe made completely impossible. Persia would have been outflanked. Even if the Germans had won the war, the Arabs believe that such is the value of the oilfields at Dhaharan and elsewhere in Nejd, they could have negotiated a peace based upon the security of the wells: for, no matter how strong the Americans may be in this area, not one drop of oil can be pumped without active Arab friendship. This cooperation could come only through the Saudi regime. But Saud had given his word.

This ultra-rapid survey of Arabian history has only noted the highlights. Ibn Saud's own life story, for instance, is one of the world's classic accounts of one man battling against odds which, as you read it, seem almost insane.

Equally, the fact that the Saudi royal family is now fabulously wealthy does not mean that they have waxed rich on oil at everyone else's expense. The very contrary is the case.

Visualize the position of Saudi Arabia in 1938, when the first royalties were coming in. Here was a country just about as under-privileged as any in the world. There were no roads, almost no electric light, no aircraft, factories, industries, banking, insurance, public security, national currency, hygiene, drainage. There was one newspaper and no radio station. Education was carried on by aged and often blind clerics, teaching small boys the Qur'an by heart. There were no building materials available except mud and a little wood. Where would you start? There was only one way to do it: Ibn Saud bought the lot himself.

He surrounded himself with all the talent that came his way. Most of those men are still with him today, and I had the privilege of meeting them. There was Sheikh Abdullah El-Fadhl, the financial brain; Sheikh Hafiz Wahba, the shrewd diplomat, and Egyptian; Sheikh Abdullah Sulaiman, from the North, in charge of economic affairs; and Fuad Bey Hamza, the Syrian, who carried the country through many a crisis.

Saud, in advising Rashid Ali against military action aimed at Britain, is on record as having said: "...I am a staunch friend of Great Britain, inheriting this friendship from my grandfather, Faisal ibn Turki. When a friend is under duress, then, for the sake of friendship, one does not act against him. Personally, if I had sufficient armaments I would have gone to the help of Great Britain and not acted against her. With the exception of the question of Palestine, Great Britain did nothing against Arab interests, and the present war is one of life and death. So our duty is, if unable to help Britain, to be neutral. This is the least that I can do."

Although King ibn Saud declared war on Germany and Japan eventually, he did not allow this to affect in the least the age-old code of Arab and Muslim hospitality. Those Arabs who had supported the Axis Powers during the Second World War and fled to him for asylum were unconditionally granted protection...

When I returned to Jeddah from Riyadh after seeing the King, I was told "off the record" of something that had taken place just before I saw His Majesty.

Someone had got the idea that I was a spy of some sort, and this rumor had reached the King's ears. Ibn Saud thundered at his informant: "This is our guest! If he is a spy, let him spy! He will not be able to combat the strength of our faith, which is the most powerful thing that we have. And if he is not a spy, as I believe he is not, then Allah will punish you with all His power, for there is no mercy for intriguers!"

But I did not know of the whispers which had preceded me to the Court, and continued my preparations to journey Meccaward, to the Shrine of the Black Stone.

CHAPTER VIII

The Shrine of the Black Stone

THE TOWN WAS full of jostling pilgrims: old and young, male and female, white, yellow and black. They thronged the old and new parts of the town, seeking provisions for the journey to Mecca, arranging transport to the Holy City, waiting for friends whom they had agreed to meet in Mecca perhaps a year and several thousand miles away.

Though quite a number of pilgrims march southward to Mecca by the austere route through the Nejd desert, by far the majority enter Saudi Arabia through Jeddah, either by sea or by way of the new and most impressive airfield. The transformation which these people all undergo as soon as they reach the holy country has to be seen to be believed. There is a saying that the Pilgrimage makes a good man better; but that it may make a bad man better or worse. Whatever the truth of this may be, there is no doubt at all that a high emotion, akin to nothing which one has felt before, grips even the most Westernized of Muslims when he sets foot even on the "secular" soil – or sand, rather – of Jeddah.

Apart from the regular flights of Saudi-Arabian Airways and other scheduled arrivals, Jeddah airport receives an endless succession of chartered aircraft from India, Pakistan and other Arab lands, even far-off Indonesia.

The actual atmosphere of the city differs little from that of many another town of some importance in the Middle East. The same fierce sun, beating down upon a mixture of modern steel and concrete office buildings with those of the Turkish and Red Sea Arab type. Open-fronted cafés, money-changers, sellers of sweetmeats and cool drinks: they are all here. There is a smaller non-Muslim population than in most Arab cities, however. One part of the city contains the magnificent foreign embassies and consulates which are not allowed to be established in the capital, Riyadh, for none but Muslims may live there, by Wahabi ruling.

It is among the pilgrims themselves that the strange otherworldly feeling exists. After the first excitement of arriving at long last on Saudi soil had passed, I made the formal vow – the *niia* – which every pilgrim resolves: and felt myself in some unique way cut off from the rest of humanity. Things like the smoking habit, like worrying about what might happen from one hour to the next, or even my future plans, all seemed to dim into a petty and more than welcome insignificance. I stopped writing my diary, found myself almost impelled by a sense of community with tens of thousands of white-robed fellows to read and recite passages from the Islamic scriptures. One felt the need for communion with a mightier, a vaster force than mankind. Although it has been said time and again that the human mind needs some sort of intermediary – whether it be a man, or a stick or stone, an idol or picture – to concentrate upon (let alone comprehend) divinity, we pilgrims to Mecca felt no such need.

We were not there to worship the Kaaba or the Black Stone. We worshipped no man, nor did we accord divine rights or a divine character to anything save one power, which we could not visualize – and did not want or expect to be able to see. Yet in us all was a feeling of contentment, an underlying excitement that we were about to achieve something which we had all worked for, to arrive somewhere which was dear to our hearts. We were on the verge of fulfillment. That was what we expected: and that was the nature of the sensation which we all experienced when we actually reached Mecca the Holy.

I sought out as many of my fellow pilgrims as I could, of diverse origins, both social and otherwise. It would be difficult to name an ethnic group, a social class or almost any other type which was not represented. Apart from the very large numbers from India, Pakistan and Indonesia (whence come the majority of foreign pilgrims) I "collected" Kurds, Bosnians, Hadendowas, Tajiks – even a Japanese. Some had been Jews, others were former Christians; there was an ex-communist who had struck up a great friendship with an extremely wealthy Indian businessman from Kenya. In our sandals and new white robes we explored the fascinating byways of the older part of the city, discussing theology and Islamic history, and exchanging stories from our lives. During these discussions, while we were waiting for our transport arrangements to Mecca, I was able to observe in some detail the change which must have come over these people since they arrived a matter of hours or days ago from the farthest corners of the world.

From what they said about their lives I could tell that some of them, not so long ago, had been of that glib-tongued, thoroughly tiresome group of Middle Eastern students who know a little about a lot of things, and have to pour it all out as soon as they are able to get it into words: which does not take long. Now, dedicated to perform the visit to Mecca and the stoning of the former idols to the north, they spoke and acted with a reasonableness which I am very sure would have surprised even their own families. There were at least three wealthy businessmen: one from Mombasa, another with textile interests in Bombay, the third a shipowner from Dacca. Different in race and tongue, they carried on their conversations in English. I am quite convinced that in any commercial contact with these men, their razor-sharp minds would have driven a bargain which no normal person could hope to match. They had that prosperous, horn-rimmed, well-cared-for look which is the stamp of the tycoon anywhere. Two of them had arrived in their own airplanes. Yet here, in the mellow Jeddah night, as we sat by the edge of the curving inland bay, their thoughts and reactions were no different from those of the gentle untutored servants whom they had brought with them. This transformation alone is to my mind one of the wonders of the Pilgrimage. Although I must admit that I was not in a very critical frame of mind, I was immensely impressed by their sincerity and calm. I never for a moment sensed any suggestion of hypocrisy, any reversion to those mundane matters which must have claimed their daily attention for upward of twenty years.

Almost as fast as they descended upon Jeddah, the pilgrims were making for Mecca: eastward to the Holy City. Like a foaming, surging tidal wave, the sea of humanity moved on and on. Barefoot and carrying packs, mounted on mules and donkeys, perched beneath awnings rigged up on camels, the poorer and more old-fashioned faithful marched. Motortrucks and buses, each one packed to overflowing with pilgrims and yet more pilgrims, glittering new American cars, monopolized the middle of the road, and threw the black, macadamized ribbon into moving, colored relief. From the devout concourse of dedicated humanity came a roar which seemed to cleave the shimmering heat-haze with almost physical force: "*Labbayk, Allahumma: Labbayk!* Here we are, O Lord, in Thy presence!"

As my car swept past the gold and green princely palaces radiating out from Jeddah's center, the emotion of the sound and movement of that almost unbelievable multitude gripped me with increasing force.

Load after load of white-robed devotees with shaven heads roared past. They were several hundred soldiers, chanting in rhythmic unison, their incisive voices momentarily gaining power over the uncoordinated prayers of the pedestrians: "*Labbayk Allahumma, Labbayk! Labbayk, la sharikalak: LABBAYK! Inna al-hamda, wa anniamata – la-ka w'al mulk! La sharikalak!*"

I felt the blood rising to my head as the accented words seized my consciousness, as it were, in an hypnotic grip: "Here we are, O Lord, in Thy presence! We are here, we are here... none like unto Thee... verily all praise... all power to Thee: Thou hast no partner!" The absolute indivisibility and possession of all power are, according to Islam, supreme attributes unique to Allah.

As the trucks swept past I noticed upon their sides the sword and date tree – emblem of Saudi Arabia. Under this is the motto, in cursive Arabic letters: "No God but Allah: and Muhammad (is) the Messenger of Allah."

In sluggish contrast to the intense movement along the motorway comes the unending white flow of pedestrian worshippers, men and women, children and nurses, guides and servants. Why do they walk? Many are poor; most, however, march this final fifty miles Meccaward either to fulfill a vow, or because they feel that greater humility and piety attach to entering the Holy City afoot as Muhammad did, nearly fourteen hundred years ago. Although a conqueror, he walked thus with the Four Companions to Abraham's shrine, there to demolish the three hundred and more idols, and to establish the worship of one God alone among the people of this land.

Stretching far away to each horizon beyond the road for most of this bleak and punishing journey nothing may be sighted beyond rippling dunes of the finest, brownish sand. Here and there a bedouin woman brings her camel to a well.

Featureless is the only word to describe the plain across which we were moving. Nothing stood out from the desert to remind us of the centuries since Arabia produced a man who was to become the inspirer of hundreds of millions. We might have been projected back into the very days of the Mission. As my faculties seemed suddenly to sharpen, I became aware of the astonishing variety in physiognomy among the surging throng. Uniform in their unstitched *Ahram* sheet, the men with one shoulder bare, there seemed to be almost no two people who resembled one another. Blond, blue-eyed chunky Syrians and Anatolian peasant types marched alongside Pathan hill-men with hook noses and curly black hair. Sudanese tribesmen, with finely chiseled features and cheek-marks denoting their origin, strode beside podgy, round-faced Indians – obviously far more used to sedentary activities. A Javanese of under five feet tall was literally dwarfed by a thin, rangy woman with copper-colored hair who was telling a ninety-nine-bead rosary of pale amber. All indications of rank or distinction, attitudes of arrogance or self-seeking, every trace of individuality, had vanished.

This was a collection of people such as even Hollywood could not hope to muster. Devoutly anxious as they undoubtedly were to reach Mecca, they were neither a rabble, nor a mere chance collection of traveling companions. This much was evident from their behavior. If one faltered, his fellows would stop and give him a helping hand. There was no wild panic when a truck overturned, and strewed its hundred occupants over the patiently plodding foot passengers. Those who immediately surrounded the vehicle stopped and picked up the bruised ones. Nobody seemed seriously hurt. Those who came behind merely made a short detour, without crowding around to see the sight. The calm would, under any other circumstances, or anywhere else, have seemed unnatural. Here I did not give it more than a passing thought.

This road is one of absolutely first-class quality, and is kept clear of sand by the incessant motor traffic: for there are no railways in southern Saudi Arabia, though the old line from the north (which was wrecked by T. E. Lawrence's Arabs) is now being surveyed with a view to putting it into commission again.

On we went, past the interminable column of humanity, as the road climbed sharply into the iron-stained foothills beyond which the Holy City lies. This precipitous part was literally hewn from the rocks by bulldozers, which are still working on the road in some places.

Through these narrow, twisting, man-made defiles climbs the car, while something like a brief gust of delicious wind seems to move swiftly past us. Suddenly, around a bend, looms a sign, inscribed in Arabic and English:

STOP
RESTRICTED AREA. MOSLEMS ONLY
PERMITTED BEYOND THIS POINT

Saudi guards, some carrying the cane switches characteristic of Nejd, others hugging automatic weapons, come forward to inspect our credentials. Small, wiry men, their martial bearing is well set off by the khaki uniform and green Arab headdress. Arranging transport, guides and a hundred and one other facilities for the half-million pilgrims is a herculean task which the Pilgrimage Administration carries out without any hitch whatever. Matters of identity, documentation and quarantine are so well attended to that I felt enormous relief that I was not trying to get past this and other posts under false pretences. It has been said that non-Muslims have penetrated into Mecca undetected. I once believed that I should have to interview such a person personally. It is not difficult to get fairly full details about the Pilgrimage, and then to write it as one's own experience. But I doubt whether anyone other than a Muslim has actually performed the pilgrimage since

Burton. While, I say, it is just possible that an impostor may have done it, I am quite sure that the difficulties today are immensely greater than they were during the time of Turkish suzerainty. Saudi Arabia has all the modern methods of detection and control at her disposal: and she uses them.

This is not to say that "a surprisingly large number" have not tried, as one police official told me...

After this point, fourteen miles from the city, the ruins of abandoned Turkish forts seem to brood in the baking desert silence. These strongpoints were raised by the Ottomans in an attempt to combat the brigand menace: but it took Ibn Saud's rough and ready justice to stamp out banditry in the Hejaz. Until the Napoleon of Arabia took over control, robber bands used to swoop down on pilgrim caravans, looting and killing.

The performing of the *haj* used to be considered such a dangerous undertaking that pilgrims, before setting out for Arabia, used to make their wills and say a final goodbye to their families. As, however, pilgrimage is one of the five essential Pillars of Islam, its performance is obligatory on all believers. The other four Pillars are prayer, fasting during the daytime in the month of Ramadan, testimony to the unity of God and the prophethood of Muhammad, and the giving of alms.

Inside the Forbidden Zone, where no life may be shed – even of an animal – we halted, to say thanksgiving prayers. Near the spot where yet another of the Turkish forts crumbles into unregretted ruin, the King has erected a shelter and well for the dusty faithful. This one was built by the hands of Ibn Saud himself; while others are now placed at regular intervals along the road.

We passed on. It could not be far now. There was tenseness visible in every face as we passed group after group of trudging figures, telling their rosaries or reciting passages from the Qur'an, which many know by heart in its entirety.

Suddenly, as we sped through the multicolored yet austere-looking igneous rocks, the dazzlingly white panorama of Mecca swept into view, spread out below, surrounded by its seven hills. The car lost speed as from the driver's lips came yet again that glad, involuntary exclamation, echoed by every pilgrim: "We are here, O Lord!"

So this was Mecca. Built in a hollow, surrounded by frowning crags, the many-storied houses have from a distance a strangely modern look. Yet the entire impression of the white stone city against the frowning brown of the crags, when seen, at any rate by a pilgrim, has something of an intoxicating quality. I distinctly remember looking at the houses, the wide streets, the carved wooden shutters, and thinking: "Here I am. No matter what happens, I have seen Mecca. I have reached Mecca. This is Mecca, the Holy..." Had I been on foot, I am sure that I would have run forward, thrown myself on the sand, made some sort of demonstration of joy. The driver had stopped the car, and was reciting the first chapter of the Qur'an: *The Opening*.

I looked back to see the effect that Mecca was having on the other pilgrims when they first glimpsed it. It may have been because of weariness, or it may have been some other reason; but the inevitable reaction to the sight of Mecca was that the pilgrim stopped dead; stood stock-still. At first there was a look of almost unbelief on every face. Then in rising crescendo came the cry: "There is no God but Allah, Muhammad is the Prophet of Allah!"

It echoed and reechoed through the gathering darkness: not a chant, not a song – both are forbidden by Islam's austere interdiction against show in religion. It was more like a cry of wonder, of hope, of fulfillment.... LA ILLAHA ILLA ALLAH: MUHAMMAD AR RASUL ALLAH...

This is the *Tauhid*, the Confession of Faith: the first Pillar of Islam. This is the phrase which should be the first sound heard by every newborn Muslim babe; the sentence which identifies one Muslim to another, the "contract" whose repetition establishes the moment of conversion of a person to the faith. It is part of the Call to Prayer throughout the World of Islam, and a part of every private or congregational prayer. It is the motto of the House of Saud, the war-cry of the Riff, the Turks, the Arabs, the Afghans. It is also one of the phrases which is used on almost every occasion, from a wedding to a birth, to death. Every Muslim is supposed to die with no other words on his lips...

The orderly mass of humanity was flooding past our stationary car now, and the driver let in the clutch, and we were off on the very last lap of a journey which had begun for all of us, in a religious sense, on the day upon which we were born.

Abundant water, drilled with the aid of modern apparatus, has made a considerable difference to the appearance of the city.

Two decades ago there was only one solitary piece of vegetation in Mecca. This was "The Tree," and pilgrims were taken to see this wonder. Today there are gardens and palm-groves everywhere. Water is usually taken for granted by Westerners and by those of us who come from greener lands. Think what a priceless boon it is in the arid East. No wonder that, realizing its value, the desert Arab may throw a few drops of the precious fluid on the sand before he slakes his thirst, murmuring, "Let the ground drink – it is more important than I!"

It is still only one Muslim in a thousand who can manage to reach Mecca in any one year; and less than one in ten (on an average) who can get there during his lifetime, even though the pilgrimage and the visit to the House of Allah is an obligation binding upon all.

After a final check of our *bona fides* we were allowed to enter the sacred city. Everywhere there were signs of modern progress: building now seems almost to be the principal industry. The available space is becoming so limited that new villas are now being constructed higher and higher up the surrounding cliffs, which in some places actually jut into the streets in the form of rugged outcrops.

Right in the heart of the city stands the central shrine of Islam: the Great Mosque and the Sanctuary of the Kaaba. Surrounded by massive walls, the place is guarded by fierce, vigilant Wahabi warriors. A vast arena is flanked by towering minarets from which the call to prayer is made, and nowadays relayed to every corner of the sacred enclosure by amplifiers. No fewer than nineteen arched gateways, richly embellished with colored geometrical designs, pierce the walls of the *Haram* – the Sanctuary. All around the many hundreds of yards of encircling rampart run quotations from the Qur'an, executed in flawless calligraphy. Photography, or the making of pictures of any kind, is absolutely forbidden by Wahabi law in this hallowed area.

Once inside, through one of those gates, the worshipper removes his shoes and walks clad only in his single cotton sheet toward the towering black-draped Kaaba: the cube, which stands in the center of the Sanctuary. The sanctified area itself is a vast, unroofed rectangle, surrounded on its inner sides by arched colonnades, resembling cloisters. Wide paths of white marble radiate from the Kaaba to the various gates.

Although there is no priesthood in Islam, the enormous numbers of foreign pilgrims who visit here without a knowledge of the customary prayers and duties have necessitated the institution of secular guides – known as *Mutawwifin.* Many of these are voluntary workers, as it were, and all of them are accomplished linguists. There are said to be a thousand such guides, who conduct the pilgrims in national parties through the ceremonies. Many are well-to-do merchants of a pious bent of mind.

I arrived in Mecca at night, and would have to wait until morning to see the Afghan *Mutawwif*, who was to be my guide.

Before starting the actual pilgrimage rite at the Kaaba, however, I decided to visit the Kaaba sanctuary.

I walked through the brilliantly lighted covered market which runs along one outside wall of the Kaaba enclosure, to the gate where the booksellers" shops are located. As I approached the gateway the rising murmur of thousands of voices repeating their prayers faded from my consciousness as I glimpsed, away beyond a line of mighty pillars, the black-draped granite cube, thrown into brilliant relief against its marble surround. Electric lighting has replaced the ancient oil-lamps of the *Haram*. Even in their harsh brilliance the immense rectangle retained that magical quality of mystery and other-worldly fascination which has been so often described by pilgrims.

I paused, wonderstruck, my senses almost reeling, certainly deeply affected. A group of newly arrived pilgrims, led by their *Mutawwif*, passed me and made their way slowly along the marble pathway toward the cube. Soon they were merged with the endlessly circumambulating figures already making their counter-clockwise circuit of the holiest place of Islam.

I made my way also toward this *Qibla* – the point toward which every Muslim daily turns five times in his prayers. As I was not yet sufficiently coached in the observances to join the actual ceremonies, I took up a reverent position some ten yards from the cube, to say the customary two prayers of thanksgiving.

Such is the breathtaking extent of the Sanctuary that this, the goal of every pilgrim heart, seemed the least crowded place in Holy Mecca. Away over to the right some two hundred African pilgrims were making their obeisances toward the Kaaba: yet they seemed to occupy an infinitesimal part of the arena.

Near the Kaaba stands the "Place of Abraham," where the patriarch is reputed to have stood to say his prayers. Formerly the Four Traditionist Schools of Islam each had its own praying-place, behind which the Hanafi, Hambali, Maliki or Shafai – as the case might be – ranged themselves. Since the puritanical Wahabis took over Mecca, these distinctions have been abolished, though the erections (rather like small archways) still stand.

A few yards farther on is the Zam-Zam: the holy well which is believed to have originated with the spring which miraculously appeared to quench the thirst of Hagar and her child in the wilderness.[3] All pilgrims drink this water. Some steep a corner of their *Ahram* robe in it, for eventual use as a shroud. Day and night these places, like the gates, are patrolled by Saudi guards with canes, alert for any infraction of customary decorum.

There was no sign of the teeming pigeons which crowd the Sanctuary during daytime. One odd thing about them is the fact that they never defile the Kaaba's covering, even though a movement among the pilgrims often causes them to wheel overhead. Neither, I was later to observe time and again, do they alight on the cube itself, though the pathways, sand, well-shelter and awnings are all covered from time to time with perching and strutting birds. These

[3]   Genesis 21:19.

peculiarities have been noted for centuries. I was as unable as my predecessors here to find a cause for this unusual behavior of the birds.

As soon as one party of pilgrims moved away from the Kaaba, another took its place. Day and night throughout the years, the faithful are always traversing this circuit, trudging round and round the Kaaba, making special supplications, intoning the appropriate prayers, kissing the Black Stone which is set in the lower southeast corner.

Many – if not all – of the residents of the city come here at some time during each day to perform this *Tawaf* ceremony.

Embedded in a silver setting in the Kaaba's actual granite matrix is the famous Black Stone. Its history is interesting, but generally much misunderstood by others than Muslims.

The Stone is kissed by every worshipper after the seventh circuit of the cube. Each time he passes it, the pilgrim raises his hands, palms outward, toward it. This attention is paid to the Stone not as an act of faith or worship, but merely because it is the only surviving relic which was touched by the prophet Muhammad, and because it was reputedly cast down from Heaven as a sign for Adam. It is said to be of meteoric origin, but I am completely convinced otherwise.

In the first place, it is not black, as I was able to see later in the daylight, but rather more of the color and appearance of dark amber. I tapped the surface, which is distinctly not stone or metallic. I would say that it is composed of an entirely unfamiliar substance which I would recognize again, but which I cannot describe by analogy. It seems to have perceptible characteristics which defy definition, but which make a characteristic impression on the eye and hands.

The heavy embroidered *Kiswa* (covering of the Kaaba) is slit at the Black Stone corner, to give access to the spot. The silver setting itself is extremely unusual in workmanship, and is shaped like an inverted bowl with a large circular hole into which one has to put one's head to kiss the Stone. In the center is a hollow several inches deep, worn into the Stone by the kisses of millions of pilgrims.

There is a story dating back to the time of Muhammad which is supposed to record one of his first indications of wisdom. When he was a small boy there was a dispute among the four important clans of Mecca as to which should have the honor of nominating a chief to replace the Stone in the place from which it had been removed during repairs to the Kaaba. Tempers ran high, and eventually – in accordance with the then invariable custom of consulting omens – it was agreed that the first person to pass into the Sanctuary from outside would be allowed to judge.

As it happened it was the young Muhammad. When the dispute was referred to him, it was expected that he would favor the candidate of his own tribe, the Quraish. Instead, he advised that one chief from each tribe should take a corner of a heavy cloth in which the stone was to be laid, so that they could share the task equally. Muhammad himself lifted the Stone into the cloth, to prevent any complications as to the right of performing this task.

This story is one of those which show that the importance of the Stone goes back before Muhammad's time. But the Stone could not have been one of the 365 idols which Muhammad later destroyed, as he would not have been allowed to permit one to survive: he himself banned anything which smacked of idolatry, and his contemporaries in the early days of Islam when idol-breaking was in vogue are on record as being of the type that would have bitterly contested any weakening from uncompromising and literal iconoclasm.

The Pilgrimage to Mecca was an established part of Arab religious duty long before Muhammad. The etymology of the city's name is traceable to an ancient word for "holy," and it seems probable that this place was indeed intimately connected with fundamental happenings in Semitic religion in times of which we have no recorded history in the modern sense.

Muhammad did not claim to be the founder of a new religion. According to Muslim belief, he merely restored the severe monotheism which was revealed to mankind through a series of prophets, of whom Jesus was one of the most important. This explains, to Muslims, why certain observances from pre-Islamic times were retained: and the same explanation is implied in the Qur'an. Unsympathetic or hostile students of the religion, on the other hand, claim that Islam was developed from Judaism and Christianity with a certain amount of purely Arabian religion retained. Needless to say, neither contention is capable of proof.

The actual rites of the pilgrimage are thus: there is the visit to the Kaaba, and its circumambulation. Then comes a sevenfold circuit barefooted between the two points known as Safa and Marwa, said to be the tombs of Hagar and Ishmael. On a certain day the entire pilgrimage sets out for a place called Mina, a few miles from Mecca, there to cast stones at three pillars which represent devils. Prayers are said on Mount Arafat, and an animal sacrificed in commemoration of Abraham's offering. The pilgrim's head is then shaved, and there is a three-day festival of dedication to a new and purer life. Anyone who completes these observances is entitled to the style of *Haji*, and generally finds that he is highly revered in his native community. In some countries, those who have made the pilgrimage wear a green turban or other indication of this distinction.

Back through the crowded streets I went to my hotel, "The Hotel of Ease and Comfort," where apartments had been prepared for official guests. Built in what seemed closest to the Moorish style, its equipment and atmosphere were altogether delightful. Servants and employers ate enormous helpings of rice and meat at the same table; in fact the dining-room had the aspect of a continuous and entirely democratic feast the whole time I was there.

My room overlooked a lush palm-garden, beyond which I could see the stately height of the Minister of National Economy's residence. I spent a few minutes in meditation on the wide, trellised veranda.

In the morning the *Mutawwif* of the Afghans called early. He was to take me and several others through the Kaaba and Safa-Marwa ceremonies. Tall, grey-bearded, robed in white with a turban tied Afghan-style, he was received with great respect by the manager and other functionaries, down to the coffee-boy.

Wearing one unstitched cotton piece around the lower part of our bodies, with a second similar sheet (the size of a large bath-towel) over one shoulder, we walked toward the Sanctuary once again, repeating after the *Mutawwif* the vow that we had made to complete the pilgrimage, and the various other prayers. I wore – like the others – a pair of sandals with the heel and instep bare. The outfit is designed to indicate decorum and humility. No other garment, no jewelry may be worn. In pre-Islamic times the pilgrim Arabs made the Kaaba circuit stark naked.

We entered the Sanctuary through the Gate of Ali (son-in-law and fourth successor of Muhammad) and walked across the sunbaked arena toward the Black Stone corner of the Kaaba, where the *Tawaf* (circumambulation) commences.

One by one we stooped to kiss the Black Stone. Then, following the guide, we started the counter clockwise circuit of the cube. The first three circuits of the Kaaba are made at a run, followed by four at walking pace. The explanation for this is said to be that Muhammad and his small band of followers ran round the Kaaba in a state of exhaustion before they were eventually allowed to perform their devotions there by the hostile Quraish. In this way they tried to show their determination and stamina.

Each time we passed the Black Stone we kissed it. When the press was too great to kiss or touch the Stone, the pilgrims raised their hands, palms outward toward it, in a gesture similar to that used when warming the hands at a fire.

Although there were a fair number of women among the pilgrim parties, men were in the majority. The women pilgrims" dress differs from that on the men, being composed of a long white dress which covers the body and arms, but with the face bare. Women are not allowed to wear veils in the Sanctuary. The veiling of women, which was to become a Muslim custom in most Islamic countries, was copied from the Christian communities in Syria by the Muslims during their conquest of that country. It was, however, known in Arabia as practiced by some of the highest class of women, and hence carried with it a suggestion of arrogance which is therefore forbidden during the Pilgrimage. In actual practice today, while the town women are veiled, those of the desert are not. White stockings and gloves complete the female pilgrim's costume. The hair must be covered. It is interesting to note in passing (since unveiling is such an issue with feminist movement in the modern East) that there is no clear injunction in the Qur'an or Traditions of Muhammad to the effect that women should be veiled. The passage cited in defense of seclusion can equally well be interpreted to mean that decorum and modesty must be observed by believing women.

Finally kissing the Stone, we moved to the "Praying-Place of Abraham," to say another thanksgiving prayer. It is at this point that every worshipper makes his personal supplication, asking Allah for that which is closest to his heart.

Abraham is said to have stood on this spot when he was rebuilding the Kaaba (which legend holds was erected by

Adam himself on the model of the Kaaba in Paradise). Then water from the Holy Zam-Zam well was brought by small boys chosen for this honor from among the noblest families. As I swallowed the liquid from the chased metal cup I noticed that it had a slightly tart taste, but was certainly not brackish or bitter, as it has been variously described.

After this part of the ceremonies, pilgrims must wait until the 8th of the month of Dhul-Hijja until they can start out on the trek to Mina and Arafat.

The rituals in the Holy City itself are completed by the run between the two small hills of Safa and Marwa, which course follows one outside wall of the *Haram*.

We therefore then left the *Haram*, and went to the starting-point of the course. After repeating the Testimony to the Unity of God (the *Tauhid*) intoned by our *Mutawwif*, we joined the throng of pilgrims running between the two points. On one side lay the mighty wall of the *Haram*, and on the other were shops mainly devoted to the sale of such items as the unique black and white rosaries which are much prized as relics of the *Hajj*.

This *Sayy* ceremony being over, pilgrims return to their lodgings or to the Sanctuary, to await the 8th of Dhul-Hijja and the expedition to Mina and Arafat.

The night before the march to Arafat, the Sanctuary's rectangular space presents the most impressive sight that one could ever see. Here the pilgrims, in their hundreds of thousands, assemble for a final prayer. Seen from one of the many high houses which overlook the Kaaba arena, rank upon rank of worshippers, bending and standing erect again, bowed from every side toward the Kaaba present an exhibition of concentrated worship which is undoubtedly unparalleled elsewhere. The same impression is again conveyed by the Farewell Visit, which takes place after the return from Arafat and the Sacrifice. During this latter ceremony, the atmosphere is charged with an electric emotion. Within a short time – perhaps a few hours, certainly not more than a day or two – the pilgrim will be on his way back to mundane affairs, back to reality, back to a life whose very existence seems to have little reality here. There is a sadness and at the same time an exultation. Both of these sensations tug at the heartstrings for long, long afterward, probably for life. Certainly I feel them still.

The expedition to Arafat is the most complicated and ritualistic part of the pilgrimage. The faithful start leaving the city for the five-mile walk to Mina at dawn on the eighth of the holy month. This exodus is even more impressive than the entry into Mecca, for this time every single pilgrim is present. Their swarming numbers resemble nothing that I have ever seen before. Almost every human being from Mecca itself is there as well. Shops are shut, streets are deserted. It seems as if the very human race itself, in its entirety, is on the move. The night of the eighth to ninth of the month is spent camping out. Visualize half a million people in the desert under canvas at one place. Can you? It is a sight which swamps the senses so that they seem able to perceive only the small, individual happenings against the sheer immensity of what is going on.

The following day the entire concourse moves off, another ten miles along the road, to Mount Arafat, and camp on the plain around the mountain. Somewhere among them, garbed in his pilgrim white, unguarded and very often unrecognized, is the King of Saudi Arabia, the Protector of the Holy Places.

Prayers are said on the mountaintop, following the precedent established by the Prophet on his Farewell Pilgrimage, made after a premonition just before his death. Then three stone pillars (the "devils") are stoned, in emulation of Abraham's putting the devil to flight when he tried to tempt him here, as the tradition has it.

The tenth of the month is the day of sacrifice, when every pilgrim must give an animal, in commemoration of Abraham offering his son as a sacrifice to God. This is the start of the Feast of Id El Adha, the Festival of Sacrifice, which is celebrated at the same time in every other Muslim country. The "devils" are stoned twice, and before the sacrifice pilgrims return to Mecca, to say a prayer in the Kaaba once more, and follow the Safa and Marwa pilgrim way. Finally, a piece of hair is cut or shaved from the right side of the head, then the entire head is shaved.

As I sat in the shaded courtyard, meditating upon these events, only the minarets of the Mosque could be seen above the towering Kaaba, with its gold-embroidered black mantle. This is the heavy damask *Kiswa*, which is embroidered with quotations from the Qur'an, and is an annual gift from Egypt. Each year the old covering is cut up and distributed among the more fortunate pilgrims, as highly prized relics. Water from the Holy Well, too, is supplied in rounded tins, and carried to the ends of the earth, sometimes to be sprinkled upon the pilgrim's grave.

Through the heat-haze I got a glimpse of the surrounding hills. All around me rested pilgrims from half a hundred countries, some telling their beads, others offering prayers. The tough-looking Wahabi bedouin guards strode alertly up and down, on the watch for any impropriety.

From the *Haram*'s administration building, with immense glass windows commanding the quadrangle, officials maintained a ceaseless vigil. I observed that the entire area of the Sanctuary was regularly swept by the field-glasses of these functionaries.

Thousand of pigeons wheeled overhead. Some traditions say that Gabriel sometimes came in the form of a pigeon, and whispered the Qur'an as it was being revealed in Muhammad's ears.

At one time pilgrims were frequently overcome by the terrific heat in this enclosed courtyard, for it sometimes reaches 133 degrees in the shade! Recently, however, up-to-date innovations have vastly improved conditions here. Electric fans have been installed in the colonnades; huge, retractable blinds shield part of the periphery from the truly burning sun. Electricity lights the Sanctuary and provides power for the Zam-Zam's pumps, and maintenance work goes on endlessly throughout the enormous area.

When I spoke to the local people about the many improvements which the King had made toward the comfort of Mecca, they often said: "Allah has rewarded him for it: was he not given bottomless wells of oil?"

Now that the actual rites of the pilgrimage were completed, I went back to the hotel to plan the photographic campaign. I decided that there would be too much risk in changing lenses so that all pictures would have to be made with the normal lens of the camera. I had originally thought of concealing the camera in a hollowed book, but this proved very difficult to do and operate at the same time. In the end I got hold of a one-pound flour bag, washed it, and made a small hole for the actual lens to have unobstructed vision. I tried to make another for the viewfinder, but this was so tricky that I decided that I would have to "shoot blind" and hope for the best.

The following day I returned to the Sanctuary, carrying my camera in the bag. Perhaps it ought to be explained that pilgrims frequently carry small cotton bags containing all their valuables or other secular things (watch, jewelry and so on) that may not be worn with the pilgrim habit.

I wanted to get pictures of the improvements recently made in the sacred area, so I first made a slow tour of the enclosure, making mental notes of things of interest. My guilty conscience did not make the attitude of the Wahabi guards or the figures in the Administration Building seem very reassuring.

When I had completed the ritual sevenfold circuit of the cube, I went and sat in the cool cloisters, where I could get a good view of the black-covered Kaaba. Slowly I sat down, looked all round, and cushioned the motor-driven camera in my hands. As I had thought, nothing could be seen through the viewfinder slit: the camera had shifted position in the bag as it was slung at my waist. Never mind. I took in the fact that the picture would include sunblind supports, electric lighting, and the Black Stone – and let off an exposure.

In the quiet of the place the sound of the motor turning seemed like a thunderclap. A guard – whom I had not noticed – gave me a look of curiosity. I decided to cough. His expression changed to one of sympathy. I seemed to be a bad case. Overcome by the paroxysm I stumbled over to the Well for a drink of water – away from the pious warrior.

After that I got a little more used to the hazards of the thing. After one shot a cloud of pigeons rose into the air and wheeled around. Soon I learned how to work the apparatus so that the shutter closed first, and by holding tightly to the winding lever I was able to prevent the set-and-wind-on mechanism – and hence the buzzing spring – from working until I was ready to cough, and to be looking in some innocent direction.

The Great Mosque, as well as being the central point of Islam, is a university. I stood at the point where the names of the Prophet and his four Companions are inscribed on a wall, to get a picture of a typical student on his way to class. I just caught an Indonesian youth, book under arm, round white skullcap and sarong, passing the inscription: when he turned right around as though by instinct, and saw me. Now this spot is just near one of the gates of the Sanctuary, and I dodged behind a pillar and then legged it out of the door.

There was nothing especially distinctive about my face or dress in this area, and I should be able to mingle with some crowd heading toward Hagar's Way.

As soon as I got outside, I saw that a group of pilgrims from, I think, India were being shepherded into the Mosque for their first visit. They had just removed their sandals, and were moving straight for me, blocking the way. If the boy was following me and I stopped, I should be caught.

The only thing to do was to do a smart about-turn, right into the middle of the advancing bunch of devotees. They made way for me, and I solemnly entered the Sanctuary with them, my little cotton bag in hand. The Indonesian had been following. He passed us, with a puzzled frown on his face.

I went out of the Sanctuary by another gate to a nearby café to collect my wits. I doubted whether the Saudi authorities would really inflict real harm upon me if I were apprehended by any of their officials. But the making of pictures is forbidden both by Islamic law (which is the rigorously applied law of the land) and by the law of the Wahabite rite. At the same time in the sanctified area it seemed far more likely that one would, if seen, be apprehended by one or more pilgrims, many of whom would be in an unusually sensitive frame of mind. Incidents of this kind have occurred.

As I sipped the aromatic tea made from green tea leaf and cardamoms, I recalled the words overheard in a Jeddah shop. "It is said that the Americans who work for the King in the North are always trying to get into Mecca. By Allah, if any of them does, he will be killed. Remember, Ahmed, what happened to that Persian who was taking photographs in the Sanctuary? And he was a Muslim, too!"

There is no doubt that I was spotted acting oddly on more than one occasion. It might have been just too bad if the people in question had realized that I had a camera in that cotton bag. Once, when I had paused to take a picture of the new metal awning which shields Hagar's Way between Safa and Marwa, I was stopped by a policeman. He seemed to me to have sensed that there was something unusual about me. He just wanted to know what my nationality was, I gathered, because there were some new quarantine regulations.

I got away with a fair number of shots on the first occasion, and developed them in the hotel. Surprisingly, many pictures show something like suspicion on the faces of people who figure in them.

Some frames – about half – were completely ruined by the fact that the blind camera had been tilted too far one way or the other during the exposure. Some were ruined by camera-shake, the bugbear of all photographers. I ruined one excellent roll of priceless negatives – close-ups of the Kaaba – through washing it under the shower, in which the cold water was hot. Almost all the unsuccessful shots I burned, and the others I rolled inside the covering of a water bottle.

I climbed the hills above Mecca to try to recapture that panorama which had dazzled me when the Holy City first swam into view from the Jeddah road. There was no point where I could get the same sort of picture without a telephoto lens. In any case all of the hillsides were crowned by houses: thousands of eyes. I did not want to start a scare, for I had heard all sorts of wild talk about how foreigners were plotting against the security of the Holy Places.

From one minaret, however, I managed to take most of the Holy Area, and a part of the rest of the city. From other rooftops I was able to photograph such things as the new hospital and municipal building. Lucky shots gave me pictures of such things as a football match under the auspices of Prince Abdullah Faisal, between those two formidable teams Mecca United and Jeddah United.

None of the pictures was really technically or pictorially perfect. My notes show that I made fifty separate forays into the Sanctuary to get a really representative bunch of pictures. Luck held all the time.

It would have been possible for me to seek special permission to take pictures of the Shrine. This has been granted before to those Muslim visitors whose school of Islam does not consider photography of objects to be forbidden by Islam. But this is unpleasing to so many pilgrims that I did not want to tour the *Haram* accompanied by armed guards. And there were further and equally compelling reasons for my hole-in-the-corner policy. I was a guest of King ibn Saud. Wahabism is utterly opposed to photography. Any application from me to the King for permission to take photographs would thus assume the nature of an insult, because I was not unaware of this attitude. On the other hand, an Arab and a Muslim is not supposed to refuse anything to a guest. Etiquette in those circles is so finely balanced that the slightest error one way or another could end in the most embarrassing results. So I had to take my pictures on my own, personal responsibility.

CHAPTER IX

Life in Mecca

IF JEDDAH GAVE the impression of a place where the East and West had come to terms, Mecca had an even more original effect upon the mind. When you first enter the city, as a Muslim, it is like descending into a vacuum. By this I mean that the experience of reaching a place which has been one of the fundamental goals of life means that some sort of fulfillment has taken place. Perhaps I can explain this best by saying that Mecca is not only a religious objective, the Pilgrimage is something more than a requirement of each and every Muslim.

Mecca is a part of history: of the almost personal history of those who belong to the civilization which grew out of one man's success story, and profoundly affected the entire world. Islam, the strict, desert-bred monotheism of a people coming straight out of the tribal atmosphere familiar in the Old Testament, swept over the civilizations – or what was left of them – in Persia, Syria, Africa and India. Then a process of selection took place. In art, science and other secular interests, Islam absorbed and adapted and synthesized streams of culture. And in the minds of the Islamized easterners, hero-worship and Arabia – particularly Mecca – replaced pre-Islamic history and to some extent national backgrounds. This process caused a telescoping of thought; even today, the history of the early Caliphate, and the detailed life of the

Prophet and his supporters, is better known to Muslims in general than their own more recent history.

This may be an ingredient of every pilgrimage. But the fact that Muslim history is so detailed and recorded with such relatively modern exactitude means that the picture seems clearer than it might otherwise be.

The process of absorption started by Islam when it came into contact with foreign ways and ideas continued as the system spread. It is sufficient in this connection to point out the total cultural assimilation of the Turkish and Mongolian invaders, who had militarily pretty well wiped out Islam as a physical force in Persia, Turkistan, Afghanistan.

Here, in Mecca today, I could see the process actually going on. There are everywhere signs of the way in which the local culture had adapted the foreign Turk to its own procedures; until now there is very little sign of Turkish influence in the Hejaz. More marked still is the present activity of digesting the Western technological impact, and integrating it with Meccan and Islamic life. Of the Eastern peoples that I have seen, only the Afghans compare with the Saudis in this respect. There is the burning desire to seize upon everything that is useful and progressive, plus the equally firm determination to sift the good from the bad, and mold all innovations into the framework of established Islam.

To what extent is this a conscious process? I had thought that it was a sort of defensive reflex – until I met Ibn Saud himself, and he told me that he was deliberately fostering this spirit as a matter of policy.

At least a hundred thousand pilgrims visit Mecca each year, from almost every quarter of the globe. The majority of them, of course, come from Muslim Asia and Africa: those very countries which are at this moment struggling to adapt themselves to the influence of the highly technical and materialistic West. The result of this vast movement of people back and forth has been that, inevitably, Muslims have taken their cue largely from Saudi Arabia.

Thus, from one point of view, one-fifth of the world's population is being constantly affected not only by the intensely religious atmosphere of Mecca, but by the attitude of the Saudi to world affairs and their development. With the recent opening of a short-wave radio transmitting station in Mecca itself, this influence is being extended far beyond those who actually attend the Pilgrimage.

The untold millions which are flowing into Saudi coffers from the Arabian-American oilfields at Dhaharan in the far northeast has made nonsense of the Hejazi's former alleged boast: "We do not need any agriculture – God has given us the pilgrims as our annual crop." The ten million pounds sterling that the country derives from travelers is but a drop in the ocean of oil money. How is the petroleum income spent?

It is said that over a million pounds has been spent on electrical and other installations, plus the improvement of the Sanctuary itself. Health, hygiene and education account for very much more.

Eight well-qualified medical officers have rid Mecca of all endemic diseases. On a surprise visit to the General Hospital at Mecca, I saw such things as the latest deep X-ray machine, flown here from America, and heard a good deal about the city's plans for a new drainage system and water in every house. The official enthusiasm for civic improvement is so high that the Government refused thousands of voluntary donations, and Emir Abdullah El-Faisal (Vice-Governor of the Hejaz) himself gave over £25,000 for water-pipes to bring additional water to Mecca.

A good deal of money is spent on the sacred obligations of social welfare and hospitality. I saw no beggars in Mecca. One obviously poor ex-pilgrim settler refused my offer of money, and I had to buy him a shirt as a gift and peace offering.

As to hospitality, during my entire stay I lacked for nothing. Day and night an enormous Cadillac was at my service, complete with driver.

Mecca's population has doubled in the past twenty years: and it is about the most cosmopolitan place one could see. Over a period of generations, so many travelers have settled here that men and women from almost every Eastern nation – in their baggy trousers, turbans, high-boots, sarongs or curly toed slippers – seem to make up the population. The number of Indonesians, Afghans and Uzbeks is enormous.

You may hear half a dozen languages in an afternoon of bazaar-gazing; eat the pungent food of India or Morocco or Iran; drink the aromatic beverages of Kabul or the spiced sour milk of Turkistan. If this sounds like a travelogue, the answer is that Meccan life is literally like this.

An abundance of large American cars has brought a traffic problem to Meccan streets – yet it is amazing how the bedouin-born policemen have mastered the art of controlling it. Car-parking, such as one may see outside Bab-Ali (one of the nineteen gateways of the Grand Mosque) is not less efficient than in any European city. When cars were first allowed to enter the Holy City I was told that drivers used more of the accelerator than was needed: "The effect of one or two rather severe sentences has been such that street accidents are not known now," as I was told by the man who offered to insure me against them for £10,000, at three shillings.

Two sides of the Grand Mosque's outer wall contain the main shopping center: the covered streets with open-fronted shops where the profusion of goods is bewildering. The atmosphere here is straight out of the *Arabian Nights* – without the inconveniences. I never saw dust, dirt, flies or maimed beggars. It is the only place I have come across where the moneychangers sit well behind immense piles of unguarded coins. The coinage, even, is interesting. The Maria-Theresa Dollar – equal to one Saudi Riyal (two shillings) – is the main currency. No notes are issued, and transactions of any size are carried out either by means of Egyptian pound notes or golden sovereigns.

It may sound like a travel agent's "plug," but I have never been short-changed in Mecca, never pressed to buy anything, never entered a shop without being treated like an honored guest.

Quite a number of shopkeepers, sages and all sorts of people – one makes friends easily in Mecca – invited me to their home for various feasts. But I had to wait, by etiquette, to salute the Deputy-Governor, before I could have any personal social life.

The young Emir Abdullah ibn Faisal was deputizing for his father – the Emir Faisal who had invited me to Mecca when I met him that day in Cairo. Protocol demanded that I should present myself to him as soon as possible, so I early ordered the car to take me to the palace.

Right inside the city an immense but austere building houses the Court of the Governor and Viceroy. Built in modern Hejazi style, with a steep flight of stone steps leading to the reception chamber, I was rather impressed by the simplicity in luxury of the place, but decided against taking a picture. After all, not only were there a number of very alert-looking Wahabis pacing up and down outside, but most of the chauffeurs standing beside their American limousines were of the special class of weapon-bearing sworn Royal Guard.

As I entered, another flight of stairs indicated the direction of the actual Hall of Audience. On each step sat a bearded, casual and uninhibited-looking warrior, some with drawn knives. Taking my name, a simply dressed Chamberlain mounted the stairs and threw open the doors. I followed him, walking straight into the immense hall where the Emir was seated with his principal officers.

There is no waiting for an audience in Saudi Arabia. Every official, from the King downward, is accessible at all times. All you have to do is to present yourself, and he is obliged by custom to see you, no matter how humble a subject you may be. The system works well, because in actual fact nobody with a real grievance will need to have it aired before the highest official: it will be dealt with speedily "out of court" to prevent the plaintiff exercising his personal right to see the Prince, alleging inefficiency on the part of a lower functionary which may cause him severe punishment.

Emir Abdullah Faisal was like a younger replica of his father. With delicate hands and feet, though not as tall, his face had the same stamp of authority, his movements the same assurance which is characteristic of the Saudi royal family.

I had a long talk with him. He spoke of the improvements to the city which he himself was planning, under the direction of his father. He pointed out to me that any facilities that I wished would be granted to me to see what I wanted, and that any complaint must be brought direct to him "at any time of the day or night."

He asked me if arrangements should be made for an audience with His Majesty in Riyadh, as a radio message had been received to the effect that I was to proceed there by one of the Royal aircraft as soon as my religious obligations had been discharged.

I asked him for a message for those who would read my books and articles. He said: "Tell what you have seen, and that we are trying to make this place worthy of Islam."

The Prince is a great sportsman. He lent me his yacht to go cruising in the Red Sea. He spoke of his plans to send a football team to Europe: for he personally looks after the interests of Mecca United, that very formidable team and terror of the Hejaz. As there are no cinemas or other places of amusement in Mecca, athletics and football draw immense crowds just outside the city on the weekly Friday holiday. The standard of their association football is extremely high.

Before I left Mecca for the north I spoke to a number of local dignitaries, looked in at the orphanage, watched scribes writing letters for their clients at the Post Office, had an all-night banquet with some Afghan friends, and was presented with a copy of the first Qur'an to be printed there.

Next to the Sanctuary is the fabulous Library, where manuscripts of utterly priceless value are kept for the use of students who travel literally thousands of miles to read records of the earliest days of Islam.

But the Prince spoke with special pride of the progress of hygiene in the Hejaz. "Make a study of it – this has never been done before," he said.

CHAPTER X

Camel Lore

IF YOU HAVEN'T been to the East, what images are conjured by thoughts of Arabia? You may say "Camels, palm trees and bedouins," or "Deserts, flowing robes and camels": but camels are likely to come into it. But how many people actually know much about camels? I certainly knew very little before I set myself to study the subject. And the betting is that you know just as little: only that the Arabian camel is larger and faster than the Central Asian two-humper.

I once asked a cat-fancier what he *saw* in felines. And almost at once there came over his face that mingled expression of fanaticism and inarticulateness that we all know so well: it is the hallmark of the devotee. The fact that one may be expected to defend feelings which cannot be expressed in words brings that desperation which so readily turns to anger. This seems to apply to any and every fanatic.

For the Arab, camels have just such a fascination. Like a cat, a camel is never actually owned, body and soul. It is a proud friend, a hard taskmaster, an utter individuality – the embodiment of couldn't-care-less. It has been said that this was why cats were regarded by the ancient Egyptians with superstitious awe: it certainly is for this reason that Arabs of all ages have believed that the camel has a special place in life. He alone, as you will know, is aware of the Hundredth Holy Name of Allah.

If you have cherished the belief that those mournful and ungainly desert ships that form an unwilling part of every zoo are true camels, you are right. But their resemblance to the milk-white racing *Dhalul*, or the lordly Kuwait fur-bearer – or any of the thirty-five recognized pedigree breeds – is only superficial.

They all have, it is true, similar physical peculiarities. That is why they are called camels. In temperament they are the same. Apart from this – well, a staggeringly enormous vista of camel (and dromedary) lore is opening out before us.

Do not believe that every camel-drover knows his job. Nobody knows for how many thousand years this has been going on, but the true bedouin, the *Arab-el-Arab*, has developed a system for the discipline and control of the animal. Any order contrary to the series of conditioned reflexes by which a trained camel operates will elicit that stubbornness which is proverbial: the bubbling and grunting, the unerring aim with the cud, lashing of splay-feet. Your camel has got out of hand.

At this state it is not recommended to seize the tail and gaily try to leap astride in the manner of King Saud's crack mountain snipers.

Those who have seen a camelman in difficulties will recall that at this stage it is generally necessary to invoke the aid of some passerby, some third party. This is thought, even in Saudi Arabia, to be because the camel has put his driver into a sort of Coventry. He will accept approaches now for a time only through an intermediary. The actual fact probably is that the casual stranger was a man who knew more about camels than the camelman. He may even be a descendant of the Prophet, which helps considerably.

Without psychiatric reeducation (which is still rare enough in Arabia, despite endlessly gushing oil royalties, to be discounted), a tough camelman is bound to be tough with his camels. This rather goes against the softer Persian dispensation, which plagiarizes the mystic Sheikh Saadi thus: "With gentle touch and language soft and fair, thou may'st conduct a camel with a hair."

Try explaining this to your unsuccessful camel-driver, and see what he says. The camel always wins: and this may be the reason why most Arabian roughs have been camelmen at one time or another. There is very little security of tenure in the job, and no opportunity to organize a closed shop except among the actual camels, who have always had one.

Here is some evidence of the response of camels to kindness – real or apparent: during two long marches by camel caravan from the Persian Gulf southward to the Hejaz, our mounts often seemed on the verge of collapse. Then I learned to whisper softly and reassuringly into my Nura's ear, and to remove a small package from her back. This evidence of good faith always worked, even if she felt the load being put back a few minutes later. It may be thought caddish by some to descend to this sort of thing. But it was the camel or me, so I readily fell into the habit. Considering that a camel is not overloaded when carrying a quarter of a ton, I do not think that my little pack could ever have been the last straw.

If you even pat a camel's neck during a long journey, he will turn his head back toward you, and gaze steadily into your eyes. You could, of course, take this as a reproach. I preferred to give it the benefit of the doubt.

On long trips, fairly fast movement – up to 12 miles an hour – gives a sense of coolness that you won't find anywhere else in the baking desert. On days where the thermometer registers over 112 degrees in the shade, the only place where you will not be scorched by the reflected heatwaves from the sand is at camel height. Even riding a horse one feels this terrible heat beating from the ground as well as from above. Air-conditioned cars, which are not rare in Arabia nowadays, will not give the same sense of coolness at all.

Five or six miles from a water-hole, your mount scents the spring, and quickens his pace; but I have often noticed that their training is such that camels will not bolt at full speed for water until given the signal. Pat him thrice on the neck, and the large soft pads will bound even over soft sand, and can reach twenty miles an hour.

We frequently used to watch the amount of water drunk by our camels, as an indication whether a sandstorm was to be expected. If he returned a second time to the pool, this was considered a sure sign of the approach of a simoom. Such a storm may well drive you almost mad in the open desert – powdery particles invading every pore, as it seems. But if you have a camel with you, you are not likely to die. Alone, hundreds of seasoned travelers are choked to death every year. Sheltering behind the camel when he sits (because he has spotted the storm long before you, of course), you can weather it. This horrible experience is followed by something about ten times worse than a hangover. But the camel will push you over as he rises, and sit grunting in fury against the storm-genii of the desert, while you drink a pint of spiced coffee from Nejd, after taking off a smog-mask made from the fine down of the northern camel.

Having now become a camel enthusiast, you have to learn the most difficult part of all: how to mount him. The camel squats, you clamber into the saddle, you give a wild shout: and he moves off. When you want to dismount, utter a strange grunt, he kneels, you get off.

If you want to know the word to make the camel do all this, you will have to go to Arabia: there are no letters, in English or Arabic, which will convey its sound and intonation.

CHAPTER XI

Locust Army

NOW THAT THE Pilgrimage rites in Mecca were over, I put in a good deal of time seeing what advances had been made in this part of the world in recent years. The most extraordinary example of this was the miracle of "Kilo Ten," on the Jeddah–Mecca road.

Here, in the middle of what was until recently parched, sandy desert, a million gallons of water are pumped each day to a little paradise of crops and fruits established by the foresight of one man – the Saudi agronomist Dr Badkuk – and the energy of his King. For thousands of years Jeddah existed on the uncertain flow from brackish wells. Frequently the people went thirsty. Until recently sea water condensation plants provided some water – on a limited scale. Today, however, there is actually a superfluity of water in Jeddah.

This abundance has brought life to Kilo Ten. The bedouin, with his apt turn of phrase, has named the settlement "The Desert's Grave" – the first indication of the fate awaiting the whole arid wastes of the Hejaz. I saw hothouses, fruits and vegetables, experimental seed wheat crops ready for distribution to farmers, irrigation channels: cool, clear water, pumped from Wadi Fatma, thirty miles away.

Three yards from this fertile patch lies what seems barren desert. Frankly, faced with the problem which Badkuk had four years ago, I would have given up. So hard have this man and his little band of helpers worked at Kilo Ten that, while the place is equipped with thermostatically controlled greenhouses, there has not been time to build permanent homes for the agriculture experts themselves: like their nomad ancestors, they live in a cluster of unassuming tents.

The second modern wonder of the Hejaz is the British Anti-Locust Colony "somewhere on the Medina Road."

Here a small group of Britishers – many of them ex-officers – maintain a lonely outpost of the Locust Service; that international organization which collects information about the insect, and exterminates them wherever they are to be found.

Equipped with all the amenities of modern science in their work if not in their huts, the anti-locust men, like their counterparts at Kilo Ten, have nothing in the nature of home comforts. Drawn up with military precision in the shadow of a barren outcrop of rocks, their camp is dominated by an enormous stack of poison bait – exactly like one of the huge slag-heaps of the English industrial north.

The Anti-Locust Service must always be mobile, on the alert. They are equipped with radio-phones, sand vehicles and repair shops. Fighting teams range over a wide area to attack the enemy as soon as he lands.

The huts are mud-walled. Instead of roofs they have canvas ceilings. This is due, as it was explained to me, to the fact that by law in Saudi Arabia no foreigner may erect a permanent dwelling. "Permanent" means with a roof. When I arrived at the camp the sun was beating down insanely upon the cluster of mud huts, their white tent-roofs sagging, as though cowed by the heat.

It was hard-baked sand hereabouts. Very little moved, and nothing grew. The tire-tracks leading to the Headquarters tent were only those of heavy-duty desert trucks. No visitors with fancy private cars ever found their way here.

At the sound of our approach a tall lean figure wielding a baton and clad solely in khaki shorts came to the doorflap of the largest hut. "If you want the Medina Road, you're twenty kilometers astray!" He came from Wimbledon, I think.

After the first slight incredulity that anyone should visit them, we went into the "Mess Room" tent, where half a dozen rangy browned figures sat, talking, smoking, playing cards. They explained that the rest of the "boys" were away on a locust hunt. The main trouble with life there was that there was often little chance to get a good crack at the enemy. By the time some bedouin had trekked into a town to report locusts, they had "come and been and gone again."

Everything here is planned on strictly army lines. Most of the officers – whose headquarters is in Nairobi and linked with the central organization in London – are former Service men.

Day and night they have a radio watch. As soon as a report of local infestation is received, reports are transmitted to the center, and mobile columns – five to ten trucks – sent out with poisoned bait and flamethrowers.

This is one of the most important centers of a worldwide fight, because the Desert Locust has been recently found to be man's worst insect enemy.

The Hejaz locust men were well abreast of world news, with special reference to locusts. I learned that not long before over 70,000 eggs were sampled in one square yard of Persian soil, that in Cyprus over 1,300 *tons* of eggs were collected and destroyed in one operation. One locust cloud can darken the brilliant tropical sky at noon for an area of 100 square miles: and, when it alights, can eat up a hundred thousand tons of food in a day.

Life in the Locust Station is hard. Apart from a few magazines and very little alcohol, there is no town nearer than Jeddah, and one would hardly choose that for an evening's spree; for Jeddah has no cinema, dance-hall or center of the type of social life familiar to Westerners.

Yet, like the men who climb mountains, or take ships for months and years into Polar regions, these pioneers are completely secure in their philosophy, self-contained in their job, and conscious, in a quiet way, of the value of the work that they are doing.

I was immensely impressed by them. The scientists and the headquarters in Nairobi will be the people who get most of the limelight, but the answer to the riddle of locust swarming and destruction may well be found here, in the desert of the Hejaz. This is the direct line of the mass migrations of the evil giant grasshopper – for that is all that it is – from Yemen and Africa to India and Persia.

Their life at times is dull: the bait-mixing, the rereading of ancient, tattered books; telling each other their life stories in their half-tent half-huts. Then, the signal and location of a swarm. Can the insects be destroyed before they take off again? Can the eggs be burnt before they hatch? Will the hoppers strip yet more precious acres of hard-won Saudi soil? There is a wild rush to get the trucks on the road: a dash of two hundred miles or more with the bait; the race to beat the hoppers to a fertile field. Then the report, as often as not:

"Hundred percent kill." Then the routine cycle starts all over again.

Many Arabs, like John the Baptist of old, catch, cook and eat the locusts, with wild honey. Bedouins – with no crops at all to worry about – think the whole enterprise is madder than just mad. Even my chauffeur thought that they were crazy, and he was better informed than most. He had been in Palestine, and having given the impression on his return that he had been to England, tried to live up to it. He defended my visit, when it became known in Jeddah, with his own theory. According to him I was not mad, just curious to see the strange group of crazy infidels in the Holy Land of Islam.

CHAPTER XII

Audience with Ibn Saud

I WAS TO leave Jeddah Field for Riyadh and the Royal Court sometime soon. When? Nobody knew. When did I buy my ticket? Tickets were not bought for the King's plane, "may your life be long..." So I just waited.

Two days later a telephone call came from the airport. Would I have my car ready at dawn, just before the first prayer, the following day? I would. Would I wait for a telephone call at that time?

Although it was midsummer, I dressed in the heaviest suit that I had, took a blanket, and packed the camera in my briefcase. With me, too, were the precious rolls of film with all my pictures on them. There is an old Persian saying: "Arabs travel with all their goods." I was not going to take the risk of losing them.

I had no idea how long I might be at Riyadh. Smoking was not allowed in Jeddah or Mecca. It must be even more forbidden in the puritanical, purely Arab, city of the Wahabi brethren. I took along two cartons of black market American cigarettes, and hoped for the best.

At dawn the telephone rang. Would I come at once to Jeddah Field? We started off in the delightful coolness of the morning along the Mecca road, with its million twinkling electric bulbs, where the unending stream of pilgrims had already been marching for some hours, taking advantage of the refreshing night air.

A man on a wonderful milk-white camel roared "Devil's Disciple!" at the dollar-grin of the Cadillac as we purred past him. Startled by the brilliance of the headlights, two Jerboas hopped aside. I felt anew the thrill of starting yet another journey, the anticipation of seeing the Napoleon of Arabia, one of my boyhood heroes...

Jeddah airport was on a scale which I found rather breathtaking at first, until I realized that every year thousands of pilgrims landed here, in their own planes, or via the Saudi-Arabian Airlines or any of the other companies which have sprung up since the Second World War.

The atmosphere was, however, unlike that of any other airport I have seen. I was weighed, my luggage was weighed, and I was given a ticket marked "Flight One, Royal Guest."

"Just wait in the lounge," said the Chief of the Airport. Here an amazingly heterogeneous crowd had gathered. The airport café is known as one of the best eating-places in the city. The smart set go to Kilo Ten for their "country outing," and patronize the airport for coffee, food and club-life. Naturally, in a climate like that, the night was the best time. During the day people who have nothing else to do sleep it off. Everybody knew everyone else. About half the hundred-odd patrons were British, American, Europeans of one sort or another. The rest were divided between stern-faced Wahabis (who were obviously passengers, and took a dim view of this revelry), and miscellaneous types of Saudi employees and gentlemen of leisure.

I got some last-minute coaching on Saudi court procedure from the Syrians who ran Jeddah Radio. Also into their group barged a nosy ne'er-do-well who had dogged my steps in both Jeddah and Mecca, asking questions and generally making himself a nuisance. According to his own account, he was a close friend of Royalty, and he was undertaking the self-imposed duty of looking after my interests. Whenever I could I gave him the slip. People who saw me talking to him – including the driver who hated him like poison – said that he merely traded on the credulity of foreigners. But I did not want to annoy him, if he were really there to look after me.

What rather shook me was his turning the conversation to photography. "Do you know anything about cameras? Do you know that when you take out the film, you have to wash it in water, and then you put into it some small beetles, which eat away the part you do not want, and leave the rest, which is the picture?" Someone must once have given him a garbled account of the effect of chemicals. I told him that I did know something about it, but I could see that I knew far less than he did.

This seemed to throw him off the scent for a bit. He stroked his straggly beard, and hitched his headdress at the angle in which it is worn by Princes. "But do you know how to make a picture to paper?" (Making a print.)

"Yes, I think so…"

He gave me a cunning look. Here was the trick question: "Then why don't you make-to-paper your pictures?"

He must have seen me developing some, or something. Anyway, I was beginning to think he could only be a sort of self-styled "prince's friend."

"Because I have nothing much to make-to-paper at the moment."

"In that case I can help you. I can get you permission to take pictures in Mecca, you would like that, wouldn't you?"

This was too obviously a trap.

"No, thank you, I have come to see the King and make my pilgrimage."

"A French woman, she came to Jeddah, tried to get to Mecca, but she was stopped. But she took pictures, and we allowed her. She thought she was clever, but we did not say anything. Then when she knew that she could take only

Jeddah, she took the plane for Port Sudan. Do you know what happened when she got on the plane?"

"No, do tell me."

"Every picture was taken away. She was a Communist!"

He skipped away on his little spindly legs, and I saw him in earnest discussion with one of the airport guards. The guard looked at me, then at him, then all round. I got up, and went across to them. The little private eyed me narrowly.

"Excuse me, Major, I understand that you are in charge of things here. I am a stranger, on my way to see His Majesty." I flashed the card. "Could you tell me when the plane leaves?"

That settled it. In a flash he had elbowed our inquisitive friend aside, and told me, with great detail, that it was necessary to wait in the lounge, and that he would see that I was collected and put aboard the plane. I did not see the shifty one again until I returned from Riyadh.

Soon I was collected and bundled aboard the twin-engined aircraft with the Saudi flag on its wings. Engines roared, the ground slipped away. We seemed to hover for minutes above the brown and white panorama of Jeddah. The usual warning signal flashed, ironically as I thought, in this land of non-smokers: "FASTEN SEAT BELTS – NO SMOKING." Nobody fastened anything – they could not read English in any case.

Women are veiled in Saudi Arabia. In this aircraft several ladies of Riyadh, muffled from head to foot in their black cloaks, were segregated in the front half. Beside me was a tribal chieftain, his jeweled sword held like a walking-stick between his knees. As we gathered height and headed northward beyond the ribbon of the Medina road, he intoned the first chapter of the Qur'an – which is sometimes likened to the Lord's Prayer, which it resembles – under his breath.

In three and a half hours we would be in Riyadh, the Sheikh told me. "See that rocky, twisting, Satan-devised camel-track below?" We were flying northeastward now, and just parting company with the Mecca–Riyadh road. "That, my brother, is the way I have traveled many a time, from north to south; yes, and south northward. Even to Palestine, by that road. It took fifteen to thirty days by camel, and five days by motor-car – if the car arrived safely at all. Now all we do is to travel by airplane, free as the winds!"

As we hummed on, over the seemingly trackless Nejdi Desert, the copper-stained hills gave way to limitless seas of sand. Grotesque, wind-eroded pinnacles of rock appeared from time to time, like the clawing fingers of the very spirit of the desert, aching to snatch us down to their level again.

Then my companion pointed to green spots appearing here and there among the parched hills. Although it was now chilly in the plane, and ice was forming on the wingtips, we could tell the sort of burning heat that beat upon the thirsty land below.

These green patches are bedouin colonies, founded by the order of King ibn Saud some twenty years ago, and now showing results. My companion was the chief of one of the settlements, and was proud of what his tribe had done in the service of the King. "Abdul-Aziz, whom I call by his own, personal name in token of my love for him, has done more than this for us." I said I supposed he meant in terms of money. "Money too, but that is only a part of it. He has given us that which money cannot buy. He has settled on the land our roving tribes, which has brought peace. There is no more bloodshed over grazing rights and water...

"During the last war, do you know what the King did? He found that there was a shortage of food among the bedouins, both settled and nomad. He brought a fleet of airplanes, and flew in all the rice and flour and meat he could find. And when that was finished, what did he do? He imported rice and flour from far afield, from America and India. He sent men to the fighting Powers, and told them that Saudi Arabia, the Holy Land of Islam, must have food in order to live. We would have that food first, and then we would decide upon which side we would fight, if at all, and how much oil we would give to the infidel for his internal quarrels."

More tortured fingers of rock, a bumpy, spine-chilling landing, and we were in Riyadh.

As soon as I got out of the craft, a red-bearded, efficient-looking military officer, in tunic and Arab headdress, stepped forward. He was in charge of the reception of guests, and he would be my "sponsor" when I was taken to the King.

First came the drive through Riyadh to the Afghan Palace, where I was quartered. Riyadh was nothing like Mecca; the architecture of the houses had something more fort-like about it. Everywhere massive walls, iron-studded doors, watchtowers. Through the streets strode dusty Wahabi "Brethren," members of the puritanical school founded by the Saudi King's own family, and renowned as the mightiest warriors of Arabia.

The Afghan Palace, I was told by the guide, was built for the visiting King of Afghanistan and his suite in three weeks. As a sign of affection, the King had ordered it to be erected alongside his own palace.

Fabulous tales are told of that pilgrimage of King Muhammad Zahir Shah: how feasting went on for days and nights, how he and the Arab monarch – both crack shots – competed at marksmanship and drew even every time; how the pious Zahir Shah amazed the Wahabi theologians by revealing that he knew the Qur'an by heart. His visit made such an impression on Saudi Arabia that I heard the saying more than once, used in connection with an admiring remark: "He is an *Afghan* of a man!"

When Zahir Shah gave valuable gifts to King ibn Saud the latter, not to be outdone, presented him with a flight of new airplanes!

This, then, was the Afghan Palace. It was a two-story concrete building, with immensely thick walls. The interior was furnished in Louis XIV style, while the bedrooms were so luxurious that there is nothing better in London. The actual building follows the usual plan of north Arabian palaces: a hollow square, with a courtyard and fountains, is surrounded by the apartments of the guests on the first floor. The servants occupy the ground floor. A cool, roofed balcony runs the whole way round the interior walls.

No windows looked out into the street. Those that there were were barred and lavishly curtained. A private telephone to the next-door palace was in the *Majlis* – the Court-Room.

I was shown to the lavishly designed bathroom, and then given a bowl of fruit and a large glass of pineapple juice from the largest refrigerator I have ever seen. I still had some difficulty in getting used to the habit of having refrigerators in every room, but in that climate it is a wonderful idea, if you can afford it.

A shortwave radio was brought and installed for my listening. The Vice-Chairman of the Arabian-American Oil Company and his legal adviser dined with me. Dressed in Arab robes, they spoke extravagantly of the courtesy and helpfulness of the King, and gave me an outline of the organization of their wells and refineries on the Gulf.

As soon as I had rested, I was taken to see the King. We crossed the courtyard, where bedouin guards presented arms, entered the wide doorway of the next palace, and moved slowly up a flight of stairs towards the Hall of Audience.

As I reached the top, I recognized the red-bearded sponsoring officer who was to present me to His Majesty.

I was just going to ask him something as we negotiated the topmost step, when I realized that we were actually in the presence of the King. There, at the end of the long double row of thrones which makes up his *Majlis* (Court), sat Abdul-Aziz ibn Saud – in a magnificent palace, no doubt, certainly regal and authoritative-looking: but no guards? There was not a single pistol, sword or knife to be seen among the servants who stood behind every seat. Ranged on either side of the King were his ministers and other celebrities. I recognized the Saudi Ambassador from London; Sheikh Sulaiman, the "financial wizard" of Arabia; the exiled blue-eyed Mufti of Jerusalem, and a host of others.

Slowly, preceded by a page and my sponsor, I walked up to the King. He could not rise, for a leg ailment meant that he was unable to move anywhere without a wheelchair, but he grasped my hand, and made me sit down next to him.

I had interrupted one of the daily news-bulletins, and waited for it to finish. Each day the powerful radio monitoring apparatus of Riyadh picks up broadcasts from various foreign stations and from this material bulletins are prepared for the King. A translator knelt on the ground before him, reading out the day's events with great rapidity. Ibn Saud listened with half-closed eyes. Occasionally he would say "repeat that," and listen again. Finally he dismissed the man, and called for coffee.

The coffee ritual in itself is an important part of Arab life. The coffee-maker advances, hands out tiny china cups sufficient for three or four mouthfuls. Then, removing his shoes at the edge of the carpet, he passes from one guest to another, filling his cup, and murmuring "may your life be prolonged." It is customary to empty the cup in not less than three "intakes," as it were. This follows a tradition of the Prophet to the effect that it is impolite to drink anything at one gulp.

The coffee we had was thin, pale golden, probably made from the husks of the Mocha bean – not the bean itself, for this is considered by some divines to be a stimulant and hence forbidden. It was flavored with the faint aroma of cardamom seeds.

If you want another cup, you allow the man to refill it. If, however, no more is required, you must not say just "no." The correct procedure is to shake the cup two or three times, from side to side. This custom arose from the far-off days when it was considered impolite for a guest to presume to order his host's servants about.

When I had kissed the King's hand, I noticed that one or two of the important sheikhs at the head of the *Majlis* turned their heads to see *how* I had kissed it. The reason for this is that if one kisses the palm of a person's hand, it is an indication that some favor is sought. Many are the tales of the King's munificence to those who have thus asked his help.

It is an actual fact that he was in the habit of giving away cars, gold watches, bags of gold and jewels, to anyone who was in genuine need and approached him. It must be remembered in this connection, though, that pride will prevent most people from asking in this way. And in Saudi Arabia, if you have lost your honor by begging, there is no way to retrieve it.

I kissed the back of his hand.

In our conversation, the King proved to be completely up to date with all current developments in the world. More so than I was myself. He spoke of international affairs, of the role of Islam in modern life, of the things that the Saudi Government was trying to do for the world in general.

"We must start somewhere; where better than in our own land? My aim, and that of all my officers, is to make this country worthy of the high destiny which Allah has called upon us as Muslims to achieve. May God grant that I have time enough to start this process!"

We spoke about a number of topics, during which I mentioned to the King that I was planning to write a book about Saudi Arabia and the rest of the Middle East that I had seen, and that I hoped that the idea had his approval. "It has my complete approval, and I congratulate you. May Allah bless you," he said.

There was a magnetism about this man that one sees but rarely. Looking at his long, athletic figure, upright and gallant even in his seventies, I could well imagine him as a mere youth of nineteen, taking almost single-handed the castle of his ancestors: the feat which paved the way for the return of the Saudi regime to Arabia.

"Your Majesty," I felt that I had to say something to account for my not having brought some present, or having accomplished something in his service. "Allah has so ordained it that that which I bring as a gift to your Throne is all that I possess: I present myself and my services to you."

The old King smiled, evidently pleased.

"My son, I accept you, insofar as you are as dear to me as my own child. And I give you yourself back to yourself, in order that you may be able to be of service to your own compatriots and coreligionists. If there is ever a time when you wish to make your home in Saudi Arabia, come and say so. It shall be done."

He made a sign to a waiting minion, and I was invested with a Robe of Honor. To receive a robe from the hand of an Eastern King is a gesture implying that one is a member of the Royal Court. I had seen my grandfather do it on numerous occasions. I knew the etiquette. Taking his hand, I tried to kiss it again, and started to kneel before him. He thrust my hand away. "Kneel only before God!"

I bowed, and after the third cup of coffee (which signifies that the audience is over) I withdrew.

The drinking of those three cups, however, took some time, during which I could watch the Saudi Kingdom at work from the top. It was remarkable how centralized was the administration. Before he signed any paper, King Abdul-Aziz would read it carefully, or have it read out to him. Some of the matters he dealt with were pleas from the simplest people who, having a grievance, merely thought that they might write to the King about it. Every one was answered.

His brain seemed as clear as crystal, and his judgment as cool as ice. When matters of intricate legal appeal were put to him, he gave judgment in a staccato voice, rich with delightful classical Arabic phrases. Almost as though it were a reflex action, his decisions would pour forth, to be taken down by scribes. Quotations from the Qur'an, case-law from the massive manuals of the Doctors of Law, illustrations and parables from the Life of Muhammad, all these, and a good deal of history besides, made up what were surely masterpieces of legal judgment. Nobody seemed at all surprised, but I could at times only look up and down the rows of grave, robed figures, astonishment probably written all over my face.

I left Ibn Saud with the rare feeling of having met a truly great man. I know that he is acknowledged as such by a large number of people probably more qualified to judge him than I: but unlike some of those, I had the priceless advantage of seeing him in action, and knowing what it is to fall under the hypnotic spell of greatness.

After that, I felt, I would have little cause for satisfaction with lesser men. If I had become disillusioned with the relatively insignificant mortals who had seemed until then people of some caliber, I felt that it was worth it. Can it not be that the price for cynicism can be worth paying? I, for one, am sure that it is, if it is a price like that. This was by no means the first king whom I had met. But it was the first man who could be – and was – a leader of leaders.

It was not long afterward that I was sitting in a Turkish café, and heard – almost with a sense of disbelief – the radio bulletin: "His Majesty Abdul-Aziz has died. As messages of condolence pour in from all over the world, his eldest son, Emir Saud, has been proclaimed King of Saudi Arabia..."

CHAPTER XIII

Saud, Son of Abdul-Aziz

IF ABDUL-AZIZ IBN Saud was the archetype of an Arab patriarchal chief, adapted to the progress – if not the ways – of the mechanical West, his eldest son is yet another and different type.

The nearest that I can get to a blanket description of Saudi Arabia's second king is to say that he could be the perfect example of the Westernized, cosmopolitan Eastern potentate familiar to English readers of fiction: only without the drawbacks. Unlike his father, he speaks a number of foreign languages with fluency and ease. His extensive overseas travels have given him the poise and diplomatic delicacy of what one imagines a perfect member of the aristocratic *élite* should be like. If you met this tall, somewhat burly, genial figure in any Western capital it would at first be hard to picture him as the soldier, administrator, religious authority that he really is.

Yet, as we talked, I could sense the power behind those steel-rimmed glasses; the clear brain working steadily and without fanaticism; the power of judgment which he focused upon even the smallest matter under discussion.

Saud, son of Abdul-Aziz, was a mature man, with his own strong personality, his own place in the administration of the country, long before the death of his father. His reputation had been won, first, in the tribal councils of the Wahabis during the period of reconstruction of the country, secondly – and equally important – on the field of battle, where he had earned the name of sharer in the conquest of Hail, and commander of tribal armies in various parts of the country.

I went to see Emir Saud in his palace near Riyadh – not that anyone could in his wildest dreams have guessed where we were, had he been projected suddenly into the place.

Leaving the forbidding walls of the capital behind, the car purred along the black shiny ribbon of macadamized road running like a sword-cut through the windblown dunes. As we neared what appeared to be a lush oasis, I watched some of the toughest-looking men I have ever seen drilling to the barked commands of a military instructor. "Halt!" The wiry, green-capped figures froze as one man. Heat-sprites danced in and out of their ranks. It seemed hotter here than the Hejaz itself. In the back row, with the other private soldiers, I noticed a Saudi Prince.

Now the "oasis" was looming closer. It turned out to be a sort of miniature forest, created, as I was told, entirely from the irrigation of a number of artesian wells which had been sunk all around it, and is situated three miles to the west of Riyadh. Through the screen of trees swept the car, up a gravel drive; and we were in an enormous landscaped garden, with all the familiar blooms of England ablaze in every color of the spectrum.

As we dismounted the horticulturist came forward, saluted, and spoke to me in Hindustani. He was an expert imported by Emir Saud for creating this garden in the wilderness.

Saud was sitting in the central chair of a long row which formed his Court, drawn up facing one side of an immense artificial lake. As we shook hands, he beamed like a rich uncle, and motioned me to the seat on his right. The other huge gilt chairs were occupied by various Saudi officials, chiefs and guests. Prominent among them was Arabia's "financial wizard," Sheikh Abdullah Sulaiman of Anaza.

The man who is now King of Saudi Arabia soon showed that he has a quality unusual in military leaders: he was completely sure of himself, relaxed, calm, almost nonchalant. Every man present listened to the jokes and light-hearted, smiling talk of Saud. Everyone knew that here was a man who could out-ride, out-shoot, out-think and out-fight any one of them: he had proved it, time and again, and could repeat the process at will. Yet, for all that, no single look of calculating thought, no sign of arrogance, no manifestation of anything other than open-minded benignity ever showed itself.

He talked of many things: of the culture of Europe and its derivations from Arab civilization in Spain. He knew about the effects of the atom bomb, of the problems of overpopulation and social security which various communities and countries were facing. He outlined part of the policy of Saudi Arabia in relation to her friends and other Muslim lands. He spoke well of Sir Winston and of the Afghan King, my own monarch. As the conversation turned to horses, King Saud ordered that some should be brought from his stable and paraded before us, in order to illustrate various finer points from life. Looking up and down the row of listeners – being myself one who has sat through many a discourse of Eastern chiefs – I never once detected any of the small signs which tell an observer that here was an experience merely being endured for an ulterior motive. On most subjects Saud held us by the force, charm and sheer penetration of his words. You might liken it to a speaker who has the "feel" of his audience, and who knows just what to say, and when to say it.

Saud speaks the most delightfully idiomatic English, too. Sometimes, when he was talking of things essentially British, he would turn to me and as he spoke I could easily picture him as an Oxford tutor: with that precise, contained and unaffected phraseology that I once reveled in at many an Oxford occasion.

Another thing that seems to mark Arabia's new king is his retentive memory. If I spoke of the new quarantine arrangements at Jeddah, he would reply with a bewilderingly detailed review of the problems and developments there. When I mentioned camels, he gave me one of the most absorbing periods of my life in describing the types, colors, sizes and breeds. Then he went on to recount classical instances of the endurance and outstanding qualities of the animal. Saud wound up by touching on the strains and his own experience in producing various types for different occupations. "The camel will never die out. It may be replaced in some spheres by a more efficient machine. But what machine gives you milk, meat, clothing, transport and companionship – and just for the cost of a little hay and water? Besides, when conditions change, you adapt your motor vehicle or other machine to the new tasks. One can do the same with the camel – by breeding. Breeding is the key to many things, and it is as well not to take up too dogmatic a view against it. It has its place. The trouble with too many people is this tendency to be unilateral about things. Look at the camel critically, by all means: but look at him constructively as well: and not only at the camel..."

I was fascinated to see the way in which this desert Prince with all the knowledge of the West behind him took every opportunity of putting a lesson, and an illustration, into what might seem at first an irrelevant topic.

As the evening came, a Wahabi elder, dressed in the simple brown robe and austere black headband of the Brethren, rose from his place, went to the edge of the pool, and called the summons to the sunset prayer. Saud rose. "Will you pray with us?"

Now the Wahabis, as I have mentioned before, are probably the most reserved of all the persuasions of Islam. No Wahabi drinks alcohol, smokes tobacco (or anything else), takes any stimulant, listens to music or wears silk. All ostentation is utterly banned. Minarets and domes on the mosques are not encouraged. Photography and picture-making come under the ban as well.

We washed our hands, faces and feet at a special fountain, and walked to the other side of the lake to stand behind the prayer-leader. The Wahabis, like other Muslims, do not have any priesthood, and anyone most conversant with the Qur'an who is available at any given moment leads the prayer.

On this occasion we formed ourselves up: grooms, servants, princes and guests – in several parallel rows facing Mecca, as the grey-bearded Doctor of Law recited a passage from the Qur'an. At prayer all are considered equal, and Saud stood in the middle of my row.

This recitation, even, was of some interest to me. Instead of the melodious wavering chant of more liberal Muslims, the Wahabis declaim the rhymed verses of the Arabic Qur'an without the slightest deviation from the normal reading. Anything else than a straightforward rendering would be considered something akin to music – and that is *Bida* (innovation), of which all Wahabis take a very dim view indeed.

In some Middle Eastern countries assassins consider the moment of prayer to be best for striking at their victim. Here, absorbed in his devotions, unarmed and off guard, he is an easy prey. For this reason kings and other important personages frequently pray with an armed guard standing in front and behind. But not Saud, son of Abdul-Aziz. The very fact of his fearlessness could be a strong deterrent to a would-be assassin.

After prayers, we entered the actual Palace of Badia, to see some of the priceless Eastern and Western art treasures which Emir Saud had collected during his journeys, or as presents. Room after room contained weapons, hunting trophies, arms and armor of the period of Islamic greatness. All were decorated in simple but perfect taste, and the value of the Persian carpets alone must have been nearly incalculable.

But the apartment occupied by the son of the desert was simple in the extreme. In one corner of an airy room was a radio set, a bureau and an easy chair. A carpet of good but not lavish design covered the floor. There were no pictures, no representation of the human or animal form: it was the Mosaic Law, carried on by Islam, against graven images.

The palace itself was not erected in any mean proportions. It seemed to me to be entirely self-contained. An electric plant provided power for lighting, refrigeration, water-pumping and the rest. Garages and stables were all separate from the huge white building, but within very easy reach. The flat roof was delicately covered with Persian-patterned wooden screens to trap the wind and deflect it throughout the palace.

I considered that it would be an abuse of hospitality to ask for photographs to be taken, either here or in the audience with Saud's father. After all, Mecca was one thing, and there I took my chance of being caught. But here I would have to ask, and the asking of something which is known to be against Wahabi beliefs – "...excused of..." but would not be expected of me. So my camera remained in its case. I had no chance to be alone, and hence snatch a picture of the palace or garden. That was that.

It was now time for dinner. I wondered whether it was to be another of the marathon feasts, sometimes lasting all night, that seemed common in the south.

But no. The table – at which about a hundred and fifty people sat – was placed on a lawn, under the cool shade of palm trees. At intervals along the grass stood electric standard lamps. The meal was entirely in European style, though with many extras in the form of side dishes of Arab and Turkish origin.

During ordinary Arab meals it is not polite to talk at all. Prince Saud, when dining in Western fashion, however, kept the conversation going with verve and enthusiasm, in three or four languages. We had delightful celery soup, fish, pilaf with chunks of lamb amid the folds of saffron-tinted rice, which the Arabs know as *Roz Bokhari* (Bokharan Rice), but which I identified as the Pathan national dish. There were all manner of green vegetables, pickled, in salad form, and cooked, as side dishes. When the chickens were brought in the Emir intimated that each man was expected to eat three chickens, and those who considered themselves weaklings and not fit to be soldiers had better stand up, and ask to be excused that number. A German medical specialist who sat in front of me – he had just flown over to examine the Prince – misunderstood, stood up for a toast, and was playfully pushed back into his seat by the overjoyed Saud. Like most Arabs there is nothing he enjoys more than a joke.

Saud is so very much like a younger edition of his father Abdul-Aziz that I could well understand Churchill's reputed remark during his wartime meeting with them that he could scarcely tell the two apart. In size, bearing and features there seemed to be hardly any difference at all. Sitting there in the garden, the soft Arabian darkness closing in on the low-powered electric bulbs, the resemblance seemed even stronger.

There was quite a debate over the book that I was going to write about this trip. Someone said that I should not omit any detail of the modern progress of the Saudi land; another felt that a fitting subject would be the growth of the country with direct reference to the King himself. All seemed well versed in the vast number of travel books dealing with the Arabs which had appeared in Europe and America between the wars and afterward.

One thing particularly noticeable about the feeling on that occasion was that – on the whole – the Saudis seemed to feel that they had not been very well done by in contemporary literature. "Travelers who write with such authority about Arabia and Arabs seldom visit Saudi Arabia, the real Arabia," said one. "They may go to Arabized areas like Syria, Iraq, Jordan, and then merely relate what the taxi driver said to them, or fill page after page with descriptions of life and wanderings, which do not seem to picture much more than the fringes of Arabia." I pointed out that, except for Muslims, nobody was really free to wander round the country. Apart from Jeddah, where almost anyone could go if he had a visa, Arabia is virtually a closed country today. St John Philby, the English Muslim writer, had published a good deal, and was writing more. There seemed no way out, since there was no likelihood that Saudi Arabia would ever be generally open to travelers.

Saud felt that, this being the case, travel writers should make it clear that they were usually not writing about the true Arabia as a whole, but about the countries of Arab civilization which bordered it. I must add here that I am positive that he did not mean this statement to be anything more than a clarification of the situation. He never showed the slightest hostility toward the neighboring Arabized lands: very much the contrary.

"It is in your hands, then," he said, turning to me. "You have been in the Hejaz and Nejd. Let us see what you can produce. I imagine that as a writer you will have a problem to know not what country to deal with, but how to treat the subject..."

This impressive experience seemed a fitting climax to the excitement of the pilgrimage. Now the Sudan beckoned, Mahdism, the Domes of Omdurman...

CHAPTER XIV

In Search of Solomon's Mines

THERE WAS SOMETHING strangely familiar – and at the same time very odd – about the atmosphere of Port Sudan. Just a short flight in an Arabian airplane, a hop across the Red Sea, and I was in another world.

The twin British and Egyptian flags of the Condominium fluttered over an orderly collection of airport buildings. We taxied to a stop, and a strapping, coal-black officer dusted the whole machine with DDT. As the door opened, and we passengers were led blinking into the harsh sunlight, a truckload of khaki-clad figures descended upon us, their shining faces wreathed in the sort of round, easy-going smile that would have been unknown in dignity-conscious Saudiland.

After a year in the Holy Land of Islam, American soft drinks, American ways and what I can only call "desert-mindedness," I experienced anew the sense of being in a British-inspired society again. Not that there seemed to be anyone from the United Kingdom in sight. Customs officials, police, white-draped idlers – all were Sudanese.

The sensation deepened in the town itself. There is a feeling of almost old-world Britain throughout the Sudan's vast million square miles that, somehow, is never incongruous.

Neatly spaced rows of buildings, towering servants with tribal slashes on their cheeks, wearing English badges on their snowy turbans, British cars driving on the left and not the right, these and a hundred other things struck me with considerable force.

I had three main objectives in the Sudan. I wanted to see the fabulous Sir Sayed Abdur-Rahman – leader of the Mahdi movement started by his father, and which is associated with the war of Kitchener and Gordon. I wanted to get the first picture, if it was possible, of the interior of the Mahdi's Tomb at Omdurman, to see something of the mines said to have been worked by minions (or genii, depending upon your attitude) of King Solomon, son of David; and there was another thing. Soon after I landed I heard that it was not allowed to take pictures in the Legislative Assembly building at Khartoum, so it struck me that it might be a good idea to have a stab at that as well.

Posed pictures had been taken, but none actually during debates. I wanted to get in somehow and give my concealed camera a chance of action. As I saw it, the Tomb was the more dangerous. Caught in the Parliament building the very worst thing that could happen would be deportation, and probably not that. But alone in Omdurman, among the enthusiastic hundred-percenters of Mahdism, one might be roughly handled, to say the least.

I decided first to take a few days off, and taste the delights of Port Sudan. Through the streets that autumn evening strolled long-limbed Sudanis, almost invariably dressed in startling white. You could tell by their turbans whether or not they belonged to the Mahdist party. Some supporters of Egypt wore the fez, and khaki, badgeless uniforms seemed to be coming into vogue as well. Indian families in their national dress made a splash of color against the biscuit drabness of the African sand. Down by the port I went for a trip in a glass-bottomed boat, fascinated by the milling multicolored Red Sea fishes that must be worth something to any aquarium.

Anyone with a movie camera and color film here could make a picture well worth while – without venturing outside the shelter of the port itself. It is whispered that certain intrepid explorers had done just that, much to the amusement of the Sudanese when the films were shown there.

It is quite a local relaxation to visit the ships from India and Aden which have called here during the day. Crowds of Indonesian pilgrims, in red and green sarongs, were welcoming fellow-countrymen off a liner packed with Australians *en route* to Britain. As a party of English-speaking tourists stopped to watch the self-inflating bluey jellyfish washed up on the shore, I raised my camera – forgetting my Arabian robes, sandals, rosary and curly black beard. "Could I have a picture, please?"

They seemed frozen to the spot. Then they all burst out laughing. They were apparently Australians: mother, father and three teenage daughters. The father grinned at me. "Who do you think you are, Cobber – Lawrence of Arabia?" I suppose something was incongruous. It must have been my English. But I couldn't help it if I went to school in England. I did not quite know whether to be annoyed or not. But I made my way back to the hotel, shaved my beard, and put on a white suit.

Here and there among the dawdling crowds of the town I saw small groups of men, striding purposefully toward the port.

Under their arms they carried a long, thick roll of camel-hair rope: the badge of the porter since the days of the *Arabian Nights*. In their astonishingly woolly hair was stuck the traditional curl-pin which showed that they were Hadendowa – the Fuzzy-Wuzzies, Kipling's "benighted heathens but damned-good fighting men" who broke the British square during the Sudan war ("because we did not know it was invincible" is the joke, enjoyed today by

Sudanese and Britishers alike in these cordial times), and have never forgotten it. These, as I had heard, were the wanderers and camel-men whom nature had deputed to surround the supposed area of Solomon's Mines.

After a good deal of thought and planning I struck northward along the Red Sea coast to look for the mines. It sounds simple, but if you have some idea of the geography you will see that it was a pretty silly idea. For hundreds of miles there is nothing but desert on one side, salt water on the other. Wells are few and far between: there is no Ibn Saud here to drill artesian wells out of apparent nothingness; no magic lamp filled with Arabian oil to conjure up asphalted roads and police the "free land" that the Hadendowa call home.

My information was scanty and my capital was small. I knew that somewhere here there lived a stubborn Irishman – and his wife – who, after twenty years of hardship, were making the mines pay. I knew that people were not supposed to visit the area. Why? You could take your pick of the reasons. The civil authorities pointed to the undeniable fact that, only recently, a truckload of rash explorers had lost their way and died in awful agony from thirst. The local civilians whispered that the Fuzzy-Wuzzies were unreliable and would fight anyone who they thought might try to open up the mines. Some people in an Arab café said that friends of theirs had tried to reach the reefs, but that their heads had been politely returned by the tribesmen, with a message to the effect that "they would always be pleased to return for burial any heads of travelers who lost their way."

The more politically minded youths whom I ran across in various offices and clubs swore (depending upon their politics) that the British, or the Egyptians, each did not want the other party to get the fabulous treasure first.

An official of the geological survey stoutly maintained that there was no gold there. No, it had not been surveyed for some time; there were no maps. There was no journalistic story there at all, only thirst and Hadendowas. No writer had ever been there.

I did not mention that I had a geology diploma, or that I had examined samples just across the Red Sea in Arabia which made me think that the workings there were complemented by Sudanese mines, because I felt that this might arouse suspicion that I was working for Egyptians, British or gold syndicates.

After a good deal of wandering, I finally came across the hundred-odd immense workings which once supplied the riches of the Pharaohs.

In spite of the unparalleled expansion of almost every form of production and industry in this land one-third the size of Europe, the mines which formerly yielded Nubian treasure for both Africa and Asia remain unworked: officially, that is.

I had searched ancient records and travel stories, made some sort of study of the ways and history of the dynastic Egyptians and the Israelites, and was fully convinced of the existence of the mines and of the riches they had once provided.

The Sudanese themselves, Nubians, Pharaohs, Phoenicians and Arabs have in turn fought and intrigued for control of the gold extraction industry. Today, working somewhere among the gigantic, six-thousand-year-old slag-heaps, was that lone Irish miner. I found no trace of him then, but met him later in a luxury hotel in Khartoum, where he was spending a holiday with his wife. He told me that things would be very much easier if local capital could be interested in the scheme for reopening mines, but money begets money so fast here in cotton that there really was very little chance that anyone would put anything into gold. He told me a good deal about the area where he worked, but for certain reasons I was not able to say that I had already been over the field.

At one place – near Dareheib – I found two slate castles probably dating from Pharaonic times, towering over workings extending many hundreds of yards. Here the gold-bearing rock still reaches a thickness of as much as twelve feet, and assays showed the comparatively high yield of four ounces to the ton. But how to provide water for the washing processes, where to get and how to transport crushing rollers, amalgamation tables? How to gain the sympathy of the hovering Hadendowa, and how to make them work for you – especially when they could, and did, do their own mining on a modest though sufficient scale? They are not a greedy people, and the offer of greater riches than they could themselves win from what they regard as their own mines would not in the least attract them.

When the Sudan and Abyssinia formed one country – the undefined up-country area of the ancient Egyptian hinterland – this and no other was the center of feverish activity to extract precious metal in response to the Emperor's incessant calls. Many thousands of slaves toiled night and day – literally, as contemporary records show – to accumulate for the monarchs of the Nile a treasure so great that, even today, it is almost incalculable.

Gold became so abundant throughout Egypt during the time of Menes, the first known Pharaoh, that the value of silver in comparison was actually higher!

Picture the scene. At some places the mine entrances are either sealed or lost, having been blocked by the Sudanese when Arab conquerors swept over the country. In most cases the towering slag-heaps – resembling those of Industrial England – stand out against both the dun-brown of the desert and the blue of the sky. Unaffected by the weathering action of the fine blown sand, the silica matrix rock gleams, here and there, with tiny twinkling specks of false gold.

Once inside one of the workings, there is something more than just eerie about the silent maze of intersecting galleries, the abandoned piles of earthenware crucibles, and the strange silence of the place.

Millions of bats now dwell in places where the preservation of even chisel markings seems to point to recent exploitation. But it is impossible that such tunnels could have been dug without literally thousands of laborers. It takes little imagination to feel, as I did more than once, that one might run across a barbarian soldier standing guard over the neatly piled stocks of perhaps fifty thousand crucibles: each one a complete replica (or perhaps I should say prototype) of those still in laboratory use, sixty centuries later.

We are fortunate in having access to detailed descriptions of the methods of work used in those days. Agatharachides, writing as late as 140 BC, tells of the period when the industry reached the peak of its efficiency.

Thousands of war prisoners and sometimes entire families slaved in the fury of near-equatorial heat under the lash of relentless barbarian mercenary guardians. He describes how the "vast numbers employed are bound in fetters, and compelled to work night and day without pause, and with no hope of escape. For they are under savage soldiers who speak a foreign tongue, and there is no intercourse possible between them."

At the site of some of these slave-camps the huts of the workers endure even to this day. Every few hundred yards the monotonous pattern of clay-built dwellings is broken by a larger and better-constructed house. In this probably lived the guardians assigned to this particular section of the slave-quarters.

Gold-mining under the Egyptians was no haphazard affair, but a highly organized industry. There can be little doubt that, due to the fact that the territory has never been adequately surveyed, many really rich deposits may exist and await rediscovery. At one time, during the earlier years of Western interest in the Sudan, companies sprang up and sought exploitation and exploration rights, but they seldom progressed far. Capitalists – at least during that time – were never marked by the pioneer spirit which would be needed almost in the nth degree to survive here.

There seems to me to be evidence that quite a number of these diggings were abandoned or deliberately blocked at various periods of history, probably on the advent of invaders. This is one explanation why the mines known at present are believed not to be those from which the greatest treasures were obtained: their yield was probably never as high as the deposits described by the ancients, or anything like as economic. It must be remembered that even slave labor can be uneconomic, for mercenary guards have to be paid, and some sort of livelihood for the prisoners must be provided. Geologists are of the opinion that natural water and food were never sufficient here to support any type of community, and hence their provision would mean something of an expense.

If, for the sake of argument, any of the fabled rich veins were to be discovered by some traveler today, there might be considerable possibilities for development. I, for one, would be more than keen to go further into this fascinating problem.

With the tunnels still intact, and some of the ancient equipment available for the using, it is not surprising that the local Fuzzy-Wuzzies carry on something of a "skeleton industry" in gold extraction themselves. Taking pieces of gold-bearing rock – which they have learned to identify – the wily warriors crush and separate them, much as their predecessors did several thousand years ago.

The Nubians of this area alone by the 17th century BC, it is recorded, were providing Egypt with a tribute of £750,000 worth of gold each year from their own mines. By the time of the Nineteenth Dynasty (in the 14th century BC) the goldmines were stated to be sending the present-day equivalent of £650,000,000 sterling annually, as Diodorus informs us in his Chronicles.

And most of this was sheer profit. The prisoners were not paid or clothed; their houses were built by themselves, "no attention is paid to their persons, they have not even a rag to cover themselves, and so wretched is their condition that all who witness it deplore the excessive misery they endure. No rest, no intermission from toil is given to the sick or maimed" – so wrote Agatharachides.

There are still mysteries surrounding the strange deserted Nubian mines. It is not known where the ancients obtained the water that they must have used. While there are some mines near the Nile banks, where water could be had in plentiful supply, yet in other places the nearest spring or well may be a hundred miles away. It is obvious that water was used; the equipment that I inspected there proves that it was indispensable to the workings, and in fair abundance for that, if not for the prisoners. Geological evidence replies that there has almost certainly not been in human times a water supply in the right part of these sandy wastes. Certainly there is nothing – here or anywhere else – to show that the peoples of those times possessed mechanical gold-ore separators for which water would not be used.

When the Arabs conquered the country in the 7th century, their own legends of King Solomon's Mines told them to look for them north of what is now Port Sudan. The apparent lack of an explanation of how the mining was done and other mysteries were clearly explained, to their minds, by the same legendary tales of the Son of David.

It is not difficult to see why. How, for example, can we explain the method of lighting a three-hundred-foot tunnel which has no indication of known artificial light being used? Unlike most of the mines of similar antiquity, there is no trace of lamp or candle carbon on the walls or roofs. Only *one lamp*, and that from a late Roman period, has ever been found: and this in spite of the fact that hundreds of relics of the time, still scattered in local profusion, include almost every other type of article of contemporary use – even down to small personal possessions such as combs.

If lamps or other artificial means of illumination were in use, it can be argued, some trace of them should remain. Elementary inspection of the underground workings showed that it would be impossible for a normal (or even, if it comes to that, abnormal) person to work along the veins without some form of portable light.

According to Arab story, the mines were actually worked by *jinn* and these genii used magical methods of lighting, and worked ceaselessly for their master, the Lord of all the supernatural beings. Comparable mines, which have been excavated in exactly the same way, are to be found in Arabia. Those that I saw there – less than two hundred miles away, just across the Red Sea – are almost identical with the Sudanese "mystery mines," and may have been worked at about the same period, and even by the same people. Historians have agreed that the Arabian (Hejaz) mines and those of Hadendowa-land may quite well date from King Solomon's day.

Having extracted the ore piece by piece, as the slaves obviously did, how did they know which lumps were gold-bearing? For they certainly did know. No method that was employed can even be guessed at. Their sorting methods were so amazingly efficient that in hundreds of tons of rejected ore still to be seen, only a few pieces containing payable gold seem to have escaped their scrutiny. Gold occurring in quartz is very often invisible to the naked eye: yet these men of Pharaoh's time found it. They knew, without powdering the rock, if it contained sufficient gold to be worth extracting or not.

As for the finished article, ancient Egyptian gold recently scientifically analyzed showed it to be 22.3 carats fine: only seven-tenths of a carat was impurities.

In the deep south of the Sudan another form of gold-extraction was shown to me in my search for Solomon's Mines. On the Ethiopian border, the Negroes pan gold dust and nuggets from the stream. They, like their fellows in the north, refer to this area as the Mines of Solomon.

The fabulous "Land of Punt" of ancient times was probably composed of the Sudan plus the countries on the Arab side of the Red Sea – Yemen and the Hejaz. When it is remembered that it was from "Punt" that Solomon is said to have received his golden treasures, a case might be made out for thinking that the Sudan mines do, indeed, form part of the group which enriched the Israelite king of old.[4]

A thousand years before Christ, the Phoenicians traded with the Sudan, Ethiopia and the Yemen. They also had, we

---

[4]   The veteran American engineer, K. S. Twitchell, speaks of the legend that Umm-Garayat Mine, across the Red Sea in Saudi Arabia, was "worked by miners of King David, father of King Solomon." He also concludes that the Mahad-Dhahab (Cradle of Gold) near Jeddah "might have been a source of the gold of King Solomon. It may possibly be called one of King Solomon's Mines." (Cf. Twitchell, K. S.: *Saudi Arabia*, Princeton University Press, 1947, pp. 160–1. On many other points of modern life in Saudi Arabia this book is very much out of date: a fact which goes to show that progress is more than ordinarily rapid there today, though from internal evidence it is likely that most of the material and photographs in the book were collected long before the publication date.)

are told, strong ties with Solomon, and worked with him in mercantile ventures.

Whatever is the truth of the matter, nothing much more can definitely be established until further written evidence is discovered.

There is nevertheless a lure about the reputed mines of Solomon that seems to tug at the mind. The urge to dig for gold probably exists in most people, and a time will come when Solomon's Mines receive attention from further prospectors. And I shall always believe that there is scope for enterprise among the silent monuments of a rarely visited area.

I shook off the magic of the Land of Punt, for it was time to journey inland, to the heart of Mahdi-land.

CHAPTER XV

Mahdism on the March

SIXTY YEARS AGO General Gordon died in the Sudan, and all England was agog as the dreaded Mahdi, religious leader of seven million people and a million square miles, threatened to sweep all Africa and the East clear of foreign rule.

Muhammad Ahmed, taking advantage of certain traditional prophecies about the "Rightly-Guided One," who was to free Islam and lead the faithful to final victory over the world, raised the standard of rebellion against Egypt in the 1880s. Muhammad Ali ("The Great") of Egypt, a man driven by a burning desire to see his country strong, revived the age-old dream of a greater Egypt, stretching from the Mediterranean to the equator, and a new Pharaonic dynasty. Some Sudanese objected to Egyptian troops in their country. Britain was dragged in as a rather less than willing participant: hence Gordon and Kitchener's expedition which seemed utterly to have crushed the power of Mahdism.

The Mahdi was dead, his family and literally tens of thousands of his followers perished on the battlefield at Omdurman. Even the corpse of the leader "on the best possible advice" was dismembered and thrown into the White Nile. The era of the Anglo-Egyptian "Condominium" had come. One thing prevented the complete destruction of the militant dervish creed. A delicate boy of ten, small for his age, fleeing southward beyond Khartoum, was spared execution by Kitchener's men. "Too young," they said. There had been enough bloodletting. Surely enough mangled corpses in their patched dervish cloaks – proud Emirs and henchmen of the Caliph – had met their doom. The destruction, if not the rout, of the Sudanese world-conquerors-designate was complete. Enough has already been written about that campaign, and I was more interested in that boy of ten.

Today that man is a multi-millionaire whose every word rings throughout a territory one-third the size of all Europe, from the equatorial jungles to the deserts of the Red Sea shore.

I left Port Sudan by air-conditioned train, traveling day and night for twenty-two hours through what seemed to deserve the name of "illimitable wastes," if anything did. Hour after hour the khaki panorama hardly changed. The most that one could see was desert, stunted acacia trees, sometimes a cluster of huts which showed a small village or station. We were getting deep into Mahdiland, and close to Khartoum itself, the capital at the junction of the twin Niles.

Whenever we stopped at a station, signs in Arabic and English would tell us, THROWING COINS OR FOOD TO SUDANESE IS ENCOURAGING BEGGARY AND LESSENING SELF-RESPECT. Nobody seemed to bother much about it, though, and tiny, appealing figures would politely hold out colored baskets "for sale." A hundred yards away the concrete beehive huts where the locals lived would be momentarily crowded by reserved elders, watching to see what luck their offspring were having with the passengers. They seemed to have plenty of luck.

A railway official in the same carriage told an amusing thing about these beehives. The railway authorities, he said, were at one time disturbed by the fact that mud and straw huts had been declared unhygienic and dangerous. As the railway is one of the all-powerful organizations here, they immediately decided upon action. The traditional type of hut was measured, weighed, surveyed – and duplicated in hygienic concrete. These beehives were then built, and exchanged with the locals for their own unhealthy homes, which were demolished and burnt. The Sudanese obediently moved in. After one day they discovered that the huts were absolute infernos inside. They seemed to let the heat in, and did not cool rapidly enough at night. So they took fresh daub and wattle and started new little villages, at a respectful distance from the awful railway ovens, which are now known as "English Hells."

Theoretically, said my friend, everyone is now happy. The official dwellings of the people are concrete huts. Their goats are supposed to live in the wattle huts. Only the goats probably feel that even the nights are getting warmer these days, as they are led into concrete houses at sunset...

I had a date with the son of the Mahdi, Sir Sayed Abdur-Rahman El-Mahdi Pasha: to his followers the Lawful Successor of the Prophet on Earth. As our train drew into Khartoum Station, a small deputation from the *Daira* (administration) of the Mahdi whisked me off the train into a large car, and toward the glittering lights of the city itself.

This first impression of Khartoum in the velvety African evening stands out in the memory with some force. Modern Khartoum, as I was soon to realize, is a town planned and built entirely from scratch on the flat open plain which is all that was left when the Mahdists took down every ancient building and ferried them stone by stone across the river to build their own capital of Omdurman.

The result is that there is nothing sordid about Khartoum. The streets are wide and well-lit. Broad avenues of Elephant-bean trees run from one end of the place to the other. A little outside the actual center of the city on the road to Omdurman lies the vast mass of the Governor-General's palace.

The car ran past this building, parallel with the Nile, and came to a halt outside a huge hotel, standing in more grass than I had seen since I left Europe. "If you want anything, please ask. You are to pay for nothing. You are the guest of the Mahdiyya," I was told.

There was nothing oriental about this place – and very little African either, for that matter. Here we were on not only European soil, as it were, but seemed actually in Britain.

Englishmen with white tuxedos and red or black cummerbunds sipped their cocktails in the palm court. Vivacious groups of British colonial civil servant types drank in the cool air and chattered on the terrace. But here, as everywhere in the Sudan, there is no color bar, and about a quarter of the guests were dressed in the flowing white gowns of the Mahdi community.

But all was not well in the Sudan. According to the Egyptians, Britain was running the country as a colony, and supporting the militant Mahdists. Egypt, they said, was not getting a fair share in the ruling of the Condominium, pro-Egyptians were being discriminated against, propaganda was being carried out against the "Unity of the Nile Valley" – some sort of unification of Egypt and the Sudan. Moreover, Egypt was not getting enough water, and the Sudan could cut off the supply when she wanted to. Control of the waters at this point – where the Niles meet – should be supervised by the country which could be literally burned up if the flow were to stop.

The followers of the Mahdi said that this was all nonsense, and that the Egyptians merely feared Mahdism because Sir Sayed could become the king of an independent Sudan. They pointed to the racial and historical differences between the Egyptian and Sudanese people. The British had not much to say, they felt that they needed most of their energies in the administration of the country. The other great Sudanese politico-religious group – the Marghanites – were against anything that was for Mahdism. Then there are the southern tribes, where men still worship trees and use razor blades for currency. Many of the Equatorial tribesmen are, however, Christians, and missionaries wanted to know if they were to be left to the mercy of the Muslim majority. The pagans and the Muslims complained that the south Sudanese had been at the mercy of the missionaries for long enough. And so it went on. I went to see Sir Sayed, to get an idea of the Mahdist mind.

Mahdism, as a system, is organized on the Arabian model. That is to say the leader is practically absolute in his decisions, and is at the same time the chief of the community in religious as well as secular affairs. His schools, youth movements, cotton-growing empire and political machine are all run from one enormous building where he also lives.

When I was ushered into his presence, ten thousand drilled disciples stood below the balcony of the cream-and-green palace. Raising the Spear-and-Crescent-Moon emblem of the movement, cheer-leaders gave the blood-tingling call that once reechoed over the battlefield at Omdurman: "One God: Allah. One leader: the Mahdi!"

Sayed Abdur-Rahman started life in exile, providing for his mother by selling wood which he collected with his bare hands and sold from door to door. His personal fortune today is estimated at six million pounds, and you can see in his face that he has tasted both the bitterness and pleasures of struggle. Knighted by the British, he was so respected by Egypt that he was granted a Pashadom by Farouk.

Sayed Abdur-Rahman (literally "Servant of the Most Merciful") is nearing seventy – which is not young for a Sudanese. He spoke slowly, weighing his words, as we sipped coffee and listened to the cheers ringing out below. Inside the palace electric fans, fluorescent strip-lighting, all the appurtenances of modernity, clash a little with the personality of the grave patriarch's appearance. But those who know him say that behind that other-worldly demure smile is one of the fastest-thinking commercial brains in history.

On the wall behind him hangs the Mahdi's sword: an heirloom taken centuries ago by one of his ancestors from a crusading German prince. If it were waved today before the endlessly marching hordes of Mahdi men, the country could be drenched with blood.

His silken robes rustling, Sir Sayed stood up to give me some idea of his plans. "First," he said, "we must have peace and welfare for the people. In the north, in places such as this" – he waved his hand toward the orderly minarets of Khartoum beyond the window – "there are few problems. Here we speak Arabic, dress in the same way, are expanding our cotton and agriculture. It is in the south, where they have no clothes, no education, no beliefs, that we must work to secure a united country."

He said nothing for or against his main local opponent, the tiny, dynamic Sir Sayed Marghani Pasha, unless this could be taken as referring to him: "When you have something to do, you must do it. It does not matter what other people say or think, if you believe in your heart that you are right. Did our Prophet worry about what the idolaters said when he had but one disciple? Did he run, or fight, when he was attacked and outnumbered by a hundred to one? Am I to model myself on any lesser man than that?"

Tantalizing glimpses of the Mahdi Empire at work were given me when I moved into the next house, at the leader's invitation.

Looming just opposite was the nerve-center of the organization: the Daira Palace. Telephones were ringing, from dawn to far into the night. White-robed clerks worked with an intensity that recalls the activity of ants. So many thousand bales of cotton from the Mahdi's own fields; so many hundred vehicles to carry exports to the ships at Port Sudan; so many books for the Mahdi Scout Leaders; a delegation to see about starting new industries; endlessly the machine whirrs.

In the blistering heat of the day, all through the fasting month of Ramadan, morning, noon and night, it went on. Was I in New York or Chicago?

Up the wide gravel pathways to the towering Daira's closely guarded gates, cars came in endless procession. Sir Abdur-Rahman's right-hand man sweeps in for a conference with cotton buyers. Government officials, Members of Parliament, religious leaders from a thousand miles up-country fill the busy waiting-halls where soft-footed servants carry sweet, thick *mazbut* coffee and pastries to the guests.

It is all like one family in the Mahdi camp. Very often I found that a number of people working for the machine in various occupations were related. Sayed Abdulahi, the present leader's brother-in-law, runs his own enormous import-export firm just a few blocks away, helped by an Oxford-educated son. Some of the key men in the Departments of the organization are sons of tribal and village chiefs upon whom Mahdism can rely to the death. Those who are accustomed to thinking analytically would be rather at a loss here. Is the Daira – is Mahdism itself – preponderantly religious? Commercial? Educational? Military? It is all of these, and a bit more. It is a community so interrelated and tightly organized that it may be unique in human organization.

Membership of the Mahdi family in the Sudan almost always means that the person must work hard within the group. He may rise far toward the top. And as such he is entitled to a tremendous amount of respect.

Sir Sayed was pleased when I told him that I planned to visit the tomb of his father across the river in Omdurman, and to pay my respects to his memory. I obtained permission to photograph worshippers before the Tomb, and laid plans for getting pictures inside, if there was any way that this could be managed. In Omdurman, the silver-domed edifice is guarded by two of the few survivors of the Battle, and they would be likely to disapprove of anyone who tried to snatch a picture of the interior: the most hallowed ground to them outside Arabia's shrines.

CHAPTER XVI

Domes of Omdurman

I GOT TO know the Qadi of Omdurman, the Muslim judge whose place in Islamic society combined religious and secular authority in matters of law. A strong supporter of Mahdism, he took me across the river to where the Mahdist stronghold sprawled: though built from the rubble of old Khartoum, the streets of Omdurman are as much a contrast to the orderly modernity of the new capital as anything can be. This part of the country is steeped in history. We passed the famous gunboat *Malik*, whose guns destroyed the Mahdi's Tomb by Kitchener's orders, now inoffensively moored beside the Governor-General's palace, and converted into a yachting clubhouse. Sturdy long-legged Sudanese, with white turbans and teeth gleaming against ebony faces, looked at us with the proud sternness that made me feel how perpetually close to the surface a man's feelings can be. No Arabian reserve or hauteur here.

At the junction of the twin Niles the judge stopped his car. "Take a photograph of the wedding of the Blue and White Niles – it should go well with your collection. It is symbolic of our country."

The ways of the East were still with us, in spite of our motor transport. We stopped at café after café, to sip tea or greet some old acquaintance, called in at the judge's mango grove to taste the new crop, talked of the future of the Sudan.

At one stop, we were just getting out of the car when the judge pulled me urgently on to the ground beside him. As I crouched low, expecting an attempt on our lives at least, thundering feet passed in a cloud of dust. As the wildly running creature dwindled away into the distance, my companion laughed. "The Governor's ostrich has escaped again."

"But doesn't anyone stop him? They can kill you, they are dangerous!"

"No, because he is the *Governor's* ostrich. He will come back eventually. In any case, he is going toward Omdurman, which is a sanctified place. Who am I to stop him?" Even religionists can have a sense of humor in the Sudan...

We picked up an enthusiastic youth, now employed by the Mahdi Daira. He had been educated by the Mahdists, and his grandfather had been a *bairakdar* (standard-bearer) at Omdurman. His excited gestures and, I thought, over-statistical mind contrasted with the quiet humor of our mellow Qadi. For the rest of the journey he spoke volubly and with blazing eyes about the four million supporters of Sir Sayed, the ten thousand graduates of Mahdist schools, the £50 million cotton crop and the £24 million now being spent upon rural uplift and development plans.

The Mahdi's silver-domed Tomb rises majestically above an immense open sanded space which is the mosque and parade-ground of the Mahdi men. Demolished by the British after the rebellion, it is only recently that Sir Sayed has been allowed to erect it again. It was, I noticed, surrounded by a stone wall and iron gates. Opposite it is the house of some members of the Mahdi entourage, containing relics of the time (the *Mahdiyyd*) and a part of the original dome from the first Tomb.

I had permission to photograph the Tomb from the outside. Then we went into the Museum, with its collections of Mahdi knives and spears, patched cloaks of the dervishes, and guns captured during the attack on Omdurman. Without thinking, I leveled my camera at one of these exhibits – a carved blunderbuss with the name of the Mahdi engraved upon the barrel. In a flash my hand was jogged. "Sorry, no photographs!" I was up against it again.

We went for lunch with one of the Mahdist Sheikhs of the town, eating the not too palatable gluey beans that are rather highly thought of, but must be an acquired taste, soup of monkey-nuts, and rice with various garnishings of vegetables and meat.

This was the day of the great demonstration before the Tomb, and the festival which follows the fasting month of Ramadan. Omdurman started to wake up. If I had been impressed by the shouting thousands before the Daira at Khartoum, I was overwhelmed by the marching and countermarching of the teeming masses of white-robed stalwarts who turned out that afternoon to sing and cheer, to group and regroup, to parade their banners from Kordofan and Nuba, from north and south, before the shrine of their leader. Everyone was there. I went to pay my respects to the Mahdi in a tent where his eldest son, Sayed Siddiq, immaculate in snowy turban, was making ready for his speech before a hundred thousand people. Sheikh El-Hindi, one of the most important leaders of the West Sudan, was there with his enthusiastic contingent, their camels and swordsmen, their banners and slogans. Only one thing was missing: music. Like the Wahabis and unlike their own opponents the Marghanists, the Mahdists consider bands and music to be bad form and irreligious.

This was an excellent chance to get to know the real leaders – at least of this community – in the Sudan. I met the hereditary King of Dongola, who now represented his country as a Member of Parliament, the Speaker of the House, Judge Shangaity, the Ulema – religious leaders – who had been with the first Mahdi on the field, and young Yahya el-Mahdi, the younger son of the chief, who was an undergraduate at Balliol. He lent me his car for the whole stay, complete with driver.

I had been "excused from attending" the mass prayers before the Tomb, on the grounds that I might be allowed to take photographs of the outside of the building. While the sermon was in progress, I climbed to the top of the Tomb (interpreting my permission rather widely) and got some very good shots of the concourse of Muslims bowing Meccaward. Then, after removing my shoes, I went into the actual interior of the Tomb.

The grave of the Mahdi is covered by a wooden, polished sarcophagus, rather to one side of the high chamber. On the other side is a large, framed banner. This is the blood-stained standard of the Mahdi himself, and on it the words:

NO GOD BUT ALLAH, AND
MUHAMMAD HIS PROPHET.
MUHAMMAD THE MAHDI,
SUCCESSOR TO THE PROPHET OF GOD.

The shrine-keeper – that venerable veteran of Omdurman – seemed to eye me narrowly. As is customary at the shrines of saints or kings, I lifted my hands in prayer, and recited the first chapter of the Qur'an.

The recitation seemed to reassure him a little, and he stood aside as I moved forward to face the sarcophagus. I could see that there was not enough light coming in through the stained-glass windows to make sure of a sharp picture: and I did not have time to experiment. It might be now or never. I had my flash apparatus in the car, and decided to go back and get it. Saluting the Keeper, I walked slowly back to the car.

This might cause quite a row. I might have got away with a hurried picture by existing light, but whatever would it look like if I went in there again, complete with a bulky flash apparatus, and started popping off bulbs all over the place?

March of the Mahdists, Khartoum

Inside the Tomb: Wooden cover of the grave of the Mahdi

As I passed them, the hundred thousand enthusiasts were deep in prayer. I did not want their disapproval to be unleashed upon me. I decided to use the element of surprise.

Five minutes later I was back at the Shrine. The aged one was nowhere to be seen, and a youthful minion let me inside the locked burial chamber. I thanked him, and knelt on the thickly carpeted floor, my back to the door. He left me to it. I took three midget flash bulbs out, put one in the gun, took aim at the sarcophagus, and pressed the button. It did not fire! Either I was in a place so holy that photographs could not be taken there, or else there was something wrong with the bulb. I took out another bulb and fixed it in the gun. It went off with a blinding flash. Still no sign of the ancient dervish.

As I raised the camera for the third time, to get a good view of the bloodstained banner, I heard the voice of the old man, muttering to himself, as he entered the precincts. Instinctively, I looked back. He was standing and looking in my direction, barely two yards away. I do not know why, but I probably could not readjust myself to changed conditions, and took the picture. The flash lighted the dim interior brighter even than that of the blazing African day.

Thoughts were chasing themselves through my mind. Would I be able to dash past him to freedom? Would a hue and cry be raised, and was the car still there for a quick getaway? Could I get the film out, and allow the camera to be taken away, and fob them off with that?

I walked to the door, and wished the shrine-keeper peace. He made no attempt to stop me.

I found out later that he was blind.

For more than one reason I decided that the time was ripe for a move, a rapid move, northward, then east to Lebanon, a tranquil land... I blessed the airplane, former object of my malice...

CHAPTER XVII

Land of the Phoenicians

IT IS FIRMLY believed by the people of the Lebanon that Noah, leaving the Ark resting upon the towering heights of Ararat to the north, brought his folk and their animals to dwell in this lovely land between the mountains and the eastern Mediterranean. Here, too, came the Phoenicians: in one of those mass migrations not unusual in the East, leaving their south Arabian homeland, they trekked to the Levant; making a new home among the glorious cedars and the snow-capped mountains.

The Lebanese Republic today is the result of a succession of historical events such as must be paralleled in few other lands. As the modern magic carpet glided over Beirut harbor, the sheer magic of the deep green sea, the gently sloping uplands, the fairy whiteness of the buildings all combined to create such an impression of sheer delight as I have never seen elsewhere. After sunbaked Omdurman it beckoned, doubly fascinating.

This, then, was one reason for the country having been a coveted prize of Greeks, Romans, Byzantines and Turks. From here the Phoenician merchant-lords directed their trading ships to Africa, Egypt and even far-off Britain. And today it is here that students of sixty nationalities come to study at the American University, in search of that knowledge whose tradition in the Lebanon has been unbroken for several thousand years.

Christianity came early to the Lebanon. Today, with a Christian majority population, Lebanon is the only Arab land where the prime minister is, by tradition, of the Christian faith. On the wide, rolling plains stretching through Tyre and Sidon southward to Palestine, nomads graze their sheep and live the placid life of a people secure in their faith, organized into clans by that patriarchal system which is unchanged since Biblical times.

Yet modern progress has come, and unashamedly. Here you will find no grudging retreat before the advance of Western inventions. Rather do the modern Lebanese – like the Phoenicians themselves – take pride in exploiting every means to make life more fruitful, more in line with a people clearly dedicated to peace.

I doubt whether there are many places as cosmopolitan as – for example – Beirut. Like most other Arab towns on the world's new highways of the air, the city teems with a variegated life, with color, bustle, men and women of a score or more of nations. In one respect, though, the city has a life all its own. Whereas in Cairo, or Athens, or even Istanbul one sees this kaleidoscope of nations as simply wayfarers, these many strange and intent figures of Beirut are native Lebanese.

Some, from the mountains, dressed in fur-lined boots and woolen cloaks, come from the redoubtable tribes of the Druze. Theirs is a heritage of war, of ceaseless guerrilla operations against the French, whose mandate expired after the Second World War, when Lebanon regained her independence.

The tall, fair-skinned athletic men in black and white turbans are the Kurds – whose origins have been traced on the wall tablets of Assyria, and who once ruled from Turkey to the Persian Gulf. Their pretender king now lives quietly in London, and Kurdistan remains split up between Iraq, Syria and Lebanon, Turkey and Persia. The main body of the people, of course, speak Arabic and dress in the Arab manner. They have their sheikhs and nobles, their black tents and herds of camels, true; yet, in spite of this, their very differences from the peninsular Arab again brings to mind the question of what is an Arab; and the only answer is that given me by a bedouin sheikh in Lebanon. "An Arab," he said, gazing at me with clear blue eyes, his massive athletic frame contrasting greatly with that of my Saudi-Arab companions, "is a man, no matter his religion or appearance, who feels that he is an Arab. Nothing more."

As I sat in a café, watching the endless passing and repassing of these exotic figures against the background of an ultra-modern city, I could not but wonder how it was that such a people – of three races and at least two religions – could combine in such harmony; working and living together, how did they feel themselves to be a nation? If this seeming miracle could be accomplished here, was there some lesson that I could learn that might provide the key to half the world's minority problems, to the unending struggle of Arab against Jew, of Muslim against Hindu, of nation against nation, that seems endemic to the present time?

I found, I believe, at least part of the answer in the famed American University of Beirut. When it was founded – as the Protestant College, some ninety years ago – its first President, Dr Bliss, laid down the principles which not only enabled this Christian organization to maintain its existence in the then Muslim Turkish Empire, but which has ever since provided the solvent of harmony in an Arab world of growing nationalistic exclusiveness.

The College decided at once that it must concentrate upon the common ground between people and peoples. It also resolved to *ignore* the differences in opinion held by the students. As Daniel Bliss said: "This college is for all conditions and classes of men without regard to color, nationality, race or religion. A man black, white or yellow,

Christian, Jew, Muhammadan or heathen, may enter and enjoy all the advantages of this institution for three, four or eight years, and go out believing in one God, or many gods, or no god at all." At the same time, the sincerely convinced Christians who founded the University were not prepared to yield on their own beliefs: "But it will be impossible for anyone to continue with us for long without knowing what we believe to be the truth, and our reasons for that belief."

Nine decades have passed since the foundation of this amazing institution. During that time, men and women of almost every nationality have graduated here; some of the past and present leaders of the Arab and Eastern world received their education at the AUB, as it is called.

As I ascended the incline through the pines and cedars to the fifty buildings which now house the University, these thoughts were in my mind. Formerly just outside Beirut, the town has so encroached during recent years that the University, with its dominant position overlooking Beirut's enchanting bay, is almost a dominating feature of the skyline. The other outstanding landmark is a colossal statue of the Virgin Mary – patron saint of the Lebanon – which rears high above the city. At night, when the crown of this immense symbol is illuminated, its effect is striking indeed.

Through the seventy acres of semi-tropical plants which comprise the college grounds I went; below, spread out maplike beside the Mediterranean foam, are the terraced slopes of gardens, running down to the vivid green of playing-fields, and then the University's own swimming beach. Beirut claims that there is no other educational institution in the world in such an idyllic setting.

I saw, chatting between lectures in the brilliant Beirut sun, students from twenty-one religious groups. Over forty nationalities are represented among the 2,700 students here.

The University is coeducational, and women as well as men travel great distances to earn the undoubted cachet of a Beirut degree. Nowadays, with the expanding East greatly in need of trained scientists, Beirut is one of the universities where the highest priority is being given to medicine, engineering and social studies. My visit to the American University was what the Americans would call a "highspot" in my exploration of truly fascinating Lebanon.

And yet – though it may be but a personal view – there seemed equal exhilaration in wandering, for a time, among the people of the countryside, talking with bedouins and traders, shepherds and soldiers, housewives and children. This, to me, seemed the most rewarding. Our delight in conversation seemed mutual; though all too often I found people of the humbler kind rather too inclined to seek *my* views, as a traveler, and not to give their own.

This politeness is something characteristic of the Lebanese and probably a result of the high tradition of ancient culture which is theirs.

Earthquakes and conquest, the Crusades and the Turkish invasion, have sadly depleted the country of its most ancient monuments. Few traces, for example, still exist of the great merchant-king Hiram, King of Tyre, who was Solomon's partner in commercial enterprises. Today Tyre as a town is nothing remarkable; yet I could not but gaze upon it with something approaching homage. It was from here that the huge merchant fleets of Phoenicia sped forth to Egypt with timber, to Cornwall for tin, to establish glorious Carthage, and to Spain, Sardinia and a dozen other places. Two thousand five hundred years have passed since that day; and though a traveler is – in the words of the greatest of all Arab travelers, Ibn Batuta – "a traveler *because* he is imaginative," I stood there, near the ruined Crusader castles, watching herdsmen bringing home their sheep, and thinking of some of man's greatest dramas enacted on this stamping-ground of the Assyrian and Babylonian hosts.

Journeying northward, again along the seaside strip, I sought out the once-famed Isle of Ruad, now little known except by its local inhabitants. Associated with Alexander the Great, it lies a few miles off the coast, and is one of the very few truly Phoenician cities to survive. Indeed, under the Phoenicians, the island, named then Arvad, as the capital of the kingdom of the same name, extended its sway far into the interior of the mainland. Bleak and forbidding even in the mellow afternoon light, it is reached by Arab sailing-boats, operated by sailors whose politeness is too great to ask the stranger's unaccountable reason for coming here.

The men of Phoenicia had brought from somewhere – with a doggedness not unusual among the ancients – vast monolithic slabs, with which to girdle the island's fortress. Many of these still stand, rising to fifty feet or more above the sea. Upon them was built a Crusader castle, which remained an unconquered outpost for a decade after the whole coast came under Saracen rule. Sallying forth from this impregnable stronghold, the Phoenicians founded a strange and nowadays almost eerie temple at Amrit, a little to the south on the mainland. Here rises the immense bulk of the "Snail Tower": a huge black cube, which represented the ancient Semitic goddess Astarte, later to be known as Aphrodite, and the Venus of the Romans. No trace now remains of the vast city which is said to have surrounded this strange sanctuary. In the gathering twilight, only the bare blackness of the cube dominates an uninviting landscape, where once great religious rites and processions must have taken place to honor the patroness of Phoenician might.

Impressive though they are, these and other ruins are distinctly alien to Lebanese life today. In Egypt, for example, when I visited the Great Pyramid and the Valley of the Kings, local inhabitants showed in their pharaonic ancestors a pride that is reflected even in modern Cairo by a fumbling resurgence of that ancient architecture. The Lebanese seem to feel no such sensation. Neither are they, in a deep sense, somehow of the West. Yet both the modern West and the oldest of Eastern Mediterranean civilizations meet here. Enigmatically, perhaps, the people of modern Phoenicia seem determined to claim something different. Their outlook on life, if I have judged it aright, tends to be focused upon cultural and spiritual progress. When I remarked on this to a very analytically minded French professor who had spent most of his life in the Levant, he held that the Lebanese mind, like that of neighboring Syria, was rooted in the wholly unique influence of the Holy Land. The pastoral and bedouin character of the people, he felt, still holds those values which were esteemed by the visionaries of the Old Testament tribes.

This may very well be true, for it is clearly not a racial attitude alone. The desert nomad of Arabia thinks very much in the same way as his fellow of Lebanon – even though they are of very distinctly different stock. I found the Lebanese delightful people, but decided it was time to head for Jordan and Jerusalem.

CHAPTER XVIII

Kingdom of the Jordan

THERE ARE TWO main pictures painted of the Hashimite Kingdom – neither of them, I found, literally true, though both combine to give some flavor of the authentic atmosphere. Those who oppose kingship, the Hashimite family or Britain claim that without the million a year British subsidy Jordan would have no separate existence. Jordan, say some, has no right to exist at all, and never has been an independent state. Why should an arbitrary strip of territory, handed out as a sort of consolation prize for the loss of Mecca in 1921, peopled by rough bedouins, be allowed to remain as a sort of subsidized British outpost?

A number of British and other foreign romantics – most of whom have never been to Jordan – picture the place as a wonderful desert land, strewn with the monuments of ancient times, and ruled by dashing Sheikhs.

Jordan is, in fact, a tourist's paradise in that she has Petra, Old Jerusalem, bedouin life, and the Roman remains in Amman. She has her back to the wall economically, because of the pitiful masses of Palestine Arab refugees who are camped on her side of the border. Lack of capital and machinery, and the problems of water and transport mean that her agriculture is not progressing rapidly enough to absorb the refugees or raise the living standards of her people.

Equally, though, there is no doubt that the country has great potentialities. Crops suitable to the climate, and some others made possible by irrigation, would create a very different picture of agricultural life, given a few more years. For progress is definitely being made, and with un-Eastern energy at that.

Like Saudi Arabia, modern Jordan first turned her attention to stopping the evil of contaminated village wells, piping the water from unpolluted wells and springs. Amman itself, once a cluster of mud houses nestling in the arms of a vast Roman amphitheatre, is as modern and progressive as any city in the Middle East.

Jordanian experts are considering the possibilities of exploiting the riches of the Dead Sea. Everyone learns at school how one cannot sink in the saturated waters of this inland lake: yet few people seem to know that the mineral salts which the Dead Sea holds are among the most valuable deposits in the world of these substances – if they were extracted.

While some processing was carried out on the Palestine side of the water during the British period, so far there is no commercial exploitation in Jordan itself.

Unlike Iraq, Bahrain, Kuwait or neighboring Saudi Arabia, Jordan has no tapped oil wells. But it is believed that the disaster which killed Sodom and Gomorrah – formerly sited here – was, in fact, a series of gigantic oil-well explosions. Part of the Government's program is to rediscover the black gold. "Then we'll show them," muttered a Jordan official to me, almost, as one might say, through his tears. It is no fun thinking of the uncounted riches of one's neighbor, and knowing that you yourself might be rich, if only there were money to do the drilling and exploration.

But most of all, Jordan is Abdullah, and Abdullah Jordan. Standing upon the steps of the new palace, gazing down at the Amman which was planned and built largely through the energy of that "little king," as he was affectionately known, I saw a small, white, unpretentious tent.

Guarded by a single sentry of the Legion, inside lies Abdullah, buried in a simple grave. A pious Muslim of the Hanifite school, this descendant of the Prophet decreed for himself an austere resting-place.

From this height one sees the whole panorama of Amman's growth; its white stone villas, the bazaars centered around the twin minarets of the city's famous Friday Mosque, which Abdullah built.

As I stood there in silent reverie, gazing into the seven valleys, I felt almost as one seeing a vision of the mind, the hopes and fears of Abdullah the Courtly. For is this not all the result of his own sweat and toil, since he entered Jordan at Maan on that fateful day in March 1921?

Many a lesser man would have broken his heart here; would have preferred to live in a more comfortable exile, dreaming of the fair Hejaz ruled by his forebears. Instead, from barren rock and waterless waste he molded a new city, a progressive State: and in the passionate fashioning of it he did not recoil sometimes from becoming a thorn in the side of East and West alike.

Thirty years ago and more, when my father sat with his friend Abdullah in the palace which is now the home of the Dowager Queen, they played chess, and the frightful difficulties ahead of the country were mentioned. Abdullah looked up, his eyes twinkling, with a serious undertone in his voice. "Do not underestimate my people. Each one of these half-million bedouins is a soldier, a farmer, a merchant, and a fashioner of a modern State." Brave words that would have appeared vain in almost any other man. Before the assassin's bullet struck him down in his own Mosque a few years ago, Abdullah had lived to see his dream come true.

Much has been said for and against Abdullah and his supposedly pro-British policies. However history may judge him, the fact remains that he, and he alone, was the architect of this tiny kingdom. In fact it seems almost as if it is his memory alone which holds Jordan together. One influential sheikh told me: "We have no nationality of our own – no history. Abdullah is what unites us, and it is his memory that tells us that we must go on, to the end of the road. And it is not so difficult, now that that great man has pointed the way. Nobody who knew him could but dedicate his life to the same path."

Abdullah a dictator? He decreed his own "abdication" from absolute power in 1950, making the Throne subject to the will of Parliament. Dictator he may have been, but he was not a tool of dictatorship.

Parallel with other national preoccupations, the Jordan Government is facing – and has been facing for years now – the living disaster of the half-million Christian and Muslim refugees from Palestine. Of these only 60,000 were receiving organized help. But for the United Nations" relief program – which means in effect a million dollars a month – almost every one of these unfortunates would have perished. But who can live on fourteen shillings per month, anywhere? I had read the words of an American journalist who, after visiting Arab refugee camps, stated that the plight of the homeless was graver even than had been that of the Jews in Europe, and I thought this a little exaggerated. After seeing with my own eyes the sufferings of these people I think that he dealt too kindly with the situation.

It is true that something is being done. Assistance, such as it is, is now uniformly distributed: but it is very thin butter on waferish bread. Sanitation, medical and social welfare services were working efficiently enough. The open-air schools and vocational training centers are impressive. As for the psychological effect of their experiences upon men, women and children, they are frankly in a most irreconcilable state of mind.

The general feeling among refugees is that both Britain and America are responsible for the eviction of the Arabs from Palestine. The adolescent youths are growing up with only one thought: revenge.

Food – somewhat naturally – monopolized most conversations. Nine and a half kilogram of flour per month did not provide even for the basic necessity of life. Officials at the camps reply that the refugees can supplement their incomes and buy rations by working outside. Since many are agricultural workers, and there are no jobs for them, this idea seemed to me to be bereft of even superficial plausibility. The United Nations has failed dismally here: and its men on the spot know this only too well. Unfortunately, it seems, decisions do not lie with them.

Numbers of refugees, it is admitted, are working on new roads and other development projects. As and when other schemes get under way, further refugee workers will be needed – if the starving wretches can live as long as that.

Private charitable institutions, like the Pontifical Mission, the Lutheran World Federation and the Muslim Red Crescent, are pulling their weight in relief work, but the sum total of their work is almost unbelievably small, compared to the immensity of the task. The general air of pessimism is shared by refugees and relief workers alike.

Can the refugees be redistributed among the various Arab lands? It is estimated that Syria can take about 350,000; Iraq another 150,000, and Jordan could keep the rest. Part of the trouble is that not all refugees want to be resettled abroad: they seek payment for the orange groves or factories that they have lost. Virtually all, as already noted, want revenge, and are hoping for a "Second Round" with Israel. Then there are those in the other Arab countries who say: "Our admitting these people will mean that we acknowledge that Israel has come to stay, had the right to dispossess them. The only condition under which they should be admitted is as temporary refugees, pending the reconquest of Palestine by the Arabs."

I need hardly say that I never met an Arab who thought that there could, or should, be peace with Israel.

But that was politics, which I never understood too well. To cool my head and fulfill a dream I had to explore Amman – then head for Rose-Red Petra.

CHAPTER XIX

Petra the Mysterious

WHEN PALESTINE CAME under British rule after the First World War, the area beyond the Jordan and east of the Dead Sea was given to Prince Abdullah, son of King Hussein of Mecca, who had rendered great services by leading the Arab Revolt against the Turks.

Emir Abdullah named his new country Transjordan – "Beyond the Jordan"; and here, in this land of Gad and Reuben, he ruled from Amman the unruly bedouin tribes who live in the ancient line of march of the Israelites from Egypt into Canaan.

Britain gave up her Mandate of Palestine after World War II, and the Jordan Arab Legion – under the Britisher Glubb Pasha – Arabia's most effective army, struck across the Jordan. At the head of the Legion and volunteer auxiliaries was Abdullah. Ancient Jerusalem, city sacred to Jew, Christian and Muslim, fell once more into Arab hands.

From the purely Arab point of view it was unfortunate that the Muslim holy place – the Dome of the Rock – should have been so easily won. This meant that quite a number of the Muslim fighters felt that, in regaining control of the Dome, they really had no war aims to accomplish. This, anyway, was what many Jordanians told me: "If Jerusalem had been further westward, we would have fought our way to the Mediterranean." In a symbolic gesture, the Christian and Muslim Arabs of the city handed Abdullah the keys of Jerusalem: "Hail, King of the Jordan!"

Today, as I walked in the colorful streets of Amman, the rock-girt desert capital, these thoughts crowded into my mind. There, within the dazzingly white ramparts of the royal palace perched high upon the mountain above me, a new young monarch – Talal, son of Abdullah – ruled. But where his father had looked down thirty years ago upon a huge deserted ancient Roman amphitheatre and precious little else, he could today see not only a truly Arab city, but the emergence of a progressive State. There is still no lack of hawk-faced bedouin nomads proudly stalking the myriad bazaars. And while quite a number of desert chieftains drive modern limousines, they will never use them in the desert; whose sunbaked sand had always struck me as ideal for motor transport. "Insult to the noble camel," they snort, when you ask them why.

Modern shops rub shoulders with seemingly prehistoric potteries, while over yonder is the immense criss-crossing of runways for the new airfield. These things, like the central heating – for the desert night is fiercely cold – have come to stay. Romance and color, dashing young officers of the Arab Legion, camel caravans and strange exotic music make up the pattern of today's Amman life.

Amman is absorbing: but two cities beckoned, with their greater mystery. In one place a single signpost with twin arrows summarized my route. One said simply "Petra"; the other "Jerusalem the Holy." I had seen each country, almost every monument, of the Middle East. Nothing, though, can approach the strange fascination of these two places: one dead yet almost throbbing with a nearly occult allure; the other, cradle of Western civilization.

And so I went, first, to Petra. For two hours my car jolted southward, through a desert wilderness whose monotony was broken only by weird wind-eroded boulders, or an occasional heavily armed bedouin, frowning his disapproval, from the proud eminence of a milk-white racing camel, for this noisy, clearly inferior machine.

Within five miles of Petra, the Hidden City, the going becomes too rough for cars. I hired a mount from the horse-dealers who have learned to wait here in the knowledge that mechanically propelled creations of the Evil One chug to a halt at this point.

Plodding uphill along boulder-strewn defiles, immense, starkly naked rocks of strange shapes rise in violent contrast to the smooth green verdure now appearing in the valleys. We entered Wadi Musa – the Valley of Moses – where tradition relates that Moses struck the rock and a spring flowed forth.

Camel patrols of the Legion pass ceaselessly here, guarding the western Jordan frontier, in the Biblical Land of Edom. Under the blazing noonday sun the effect is most impressive: the intermingling reds, blues, greens of the rocks, a white foaming brook, the tough-bearded Legionaries in Arab headdress. Thus may this land have looked at almost any time during the past four thousand years.

On, twisting through the two-hour labyrinth between the mountain of Seir, we came upon groups of small brown and white hillocks. These are the reputed tombs of the Guardians of Petra, the invulnerable city. Then, as though split by some gigantic chisel, a jagged cleft in the towering cliffs shows the only path through which the rock-hewn city can be entered.

Amazing though it may seem, Petra is invisible until you are almost upon it. Wall upon wall of native stone, rampart after rampart rises in seeming chaos. "Allah laughed when he threw these mountains down here," chuckled my bedouin guide. Yet beyond these towering walls, through the single cleft called the *Sik*, lies the wondrous Nabataen city.

This is Petra: inside the grim mountain-mass, as though the center has been scooped out, lies a valley, actually fifteen square miles in area. On every side of this hidden depression magnificent façades have been hewn, over a period of centuries. Immense colonnaded cloisters, vast pillared halls, arched and arcaded treasuries, audience-halls, temples and a hundred other edifices loom like a fairy city. Yet the only entrance to this wonderland is that narrow split between the mountains, and every single building has been carved out by hand *in situ*, in a variety of styles, of which the predominant motifs are classical Greek. Add to all this the fact that the rocks are of every shade of red, and the façades of gargantuan size, and you will have some idea of the breathtaking glory of the dead – but somehow almost living – city of Petra.

What is its story? As in many other things, the Bible tells us something of it. When Jacob, expelling the Horites from their rocky fastnesses, gave Esau his chance to come here, the people were known after this as Edomites:

"The pride of thine heart hath deceived thee, thou that dwellest in the clefts of the rock, whose habitation is high; that saith in his heart, Who shall bring me down to the ground?" (Obadiah, v. 3.)

It was the Edomites, the ancient Petrans, who refused the Israelites passage when they returned this way from the Egyptian captivity. It is believed that thirst came upon the Israelites near Petra, and Moses struck the rock here: hence the Valley of Moses. This stream still runs, and is still believed by the local people to possess miraculous properties.

The Edomites and Israelites never became harmonized. Extending their sway up to the Jordan River, the men of Edom were in their turn replaced by the Nabataens, a highly cultured Arab tribe. Divided into two sections – soldiers and merchants – they traded, it is said, with distant China, and their inscriptions have been found as far afield as Italy.

Fighting the Romans for centuries, it was only in AD 106 that they were overcome. From that date they disappeared, and history is mute about Petra until the Crusaders came and built here their church, the only building not hewn from the rocks.

As I rode into the secret city, I noticed that the narrow stone walls on either side of the cleft were worn smooth by erosion or human passage through past uncounted centuries. The oblique sunlight strikes reddish-brown against the rocks. From here there is a sheer drop of nearly seven hundred feet. Easy to defend, it is almost impossible to conceive how this place could have been taken in war. Treachery seems the answer. As my horse picked his way gingerly along the ledge, a whispering echo of the wind was all that broke into my silent reflections.

After a mile of this comes the first, and most gorgeous, façade of all: the Treasury, which marks the beginning of the valley. The blazing sun's rays, pouring into the now open cup-shaped valley, heightens a glowing illusion of red-hotness over the whole area. Within the massive portals, like other Petra chambers, there is nothing now to relieve the vast emptiness of the interior. No furniture, nothing but all-pervading solitude, in what was once the center of a mighty empire. Local legend says, however, that the Nabataen merchant-princes, "Each with five to ten hundred slaves, lay upon costly inlaid ivory divans; gold and silver were their platters, even of the lesser people; the rich carpets lay seven deep upon the floors."

The soldiers, though, seem to have lived a more austere life than that. I went into one guard-house at the entrance of the Treasury. Across the center of the room was a wide stone table, flanked by narrow, smooth rock-hewn benches. The Nabataens must have been small people, for I found it uncomfortable to fit myself between the seat and the table.

Beyond this, the valley opens out. On the right and left lie tombs and halls (one the great Hall of Audience of the ancient kings), each one decorated outside with intricate carving, statues and columns. The detail still remains, every inch a monument to man's creative skill.

Literally hundreds of tombs, altars and sacrificial places are cut in the variegated rose-red and terracotta rocks. Inside, as outside, the veins of green, red, yellow and blue sandstone give a gorgeous effect, a warm reaction of almost physical well-being: akin to the enjoyment of inlaid precious stones.

And, when the night falls, and the moon rides the skies and this fairy city is bathed in her silvery light, there is such a blending of subtle color on the faces of the rock-temples, contrasting with the massive solidity of the carving, as to beggar description.

Two thousand years and more seemed to roll back as I trod this strange place, and the imagination conjured up living scenes in every wonder. The long-robed priests of the Sun-god Dushara at the Altar of Sacrifice; the golden-helmeted officers of the Imperial Guard; the hoard of priceless gems still locally believed to be hidden in the huge but inaccessible stone urn surmounting the Treasury.

The oddest thing about those civilized savages who must have been the Nabataens of Petra was their eagerness to adopt anything and everything from those with whom they came in contact. They worshipped the stellar gods of their Arab ancestors, looted and traded far and wide to bring both wealth and architectural ideas to their bandit kingdom.

Even when the Emperor Trajan finally gained the city for Rome, the Petrans avidly copied his architecture for their rock palaces. Even the Roman conquest did not finish Petra. A vast amphitheater was hewn out of the rock, and life must have gone on very much as before, the guardians of this strategic point continuing to levy tribute upon the luckless caravans wending their way to Mecca and South Arabia.

But the drift of trade and economy strangled the robber fortress. To my mind it should be considered one of the wonders of the world. I doubt if anyone could even glimpse that seventy-foot-high cleft which is the entrance without feeling a thrill of regret that this civilization should have passed away.

But such is human restlessness that I retraced my steps toward Amman, for the lure of that other goal was now tugging at my thoughts: Jerusalem the Holy...

CHAPTER XX

The Rock of Paradise

STANDING NOT FAR from the Chapel of the Ascension, on the Mount of Olives, looking down upon the panorama of religions that is Jerusalem, I began to feel some inkling of the unity in diversity that here almost speaks aloud of man's striving toward the infinite.

Towering above the city's skyline was what I had really come to see: the Dome of the Rock, second holiest place of Islam after Mecca, built upon the site of Solomon's Temple. Beyond that, less well-defined, blocks of houses forming David Street carry the gaze as far as Notre Dame de France; and past it, like a pure white silky ribbon, snakes the Jaffa road, patrolled by Legion armored cars, mere dots they seemed from where I stood.

The Dome of the Rock must be one of the world's most extraordinary buildings, both in actual fact and in mythical attribution. Over a vast paved courtyard rises this many-sided Shrine, with its plain, impressive dome housing the Rock which legend claims to be one of the foundations of Paradise. The present building was put up by the Caliph Abd-el-Malik, at a cost equal to seven years" revenue of all Egypt. It is revered by the Jews, Christians and Muslims alike, and must be one of the earliest sites of man's consecration to the ideal of a Single God.

It is here that the Jews resorted to bemoan their fate, and one side of the place is that which is known as the Wailing

Wall. It was one of the most hotly contested holy places during the Crusades, and Baldwin II converted it into a church. It was the original Temple of the Order of Knights Templar.

Tradition says that the Chaldeans destroyed Solomon's Temple on this site, and that the Rock itself (which is still visible within the Shrine) was the Throne of the son of David himself. Seventy years later it was rebuilt, only to be leveled again. Herod repaired it, and turned it over to the Jews. Jesus was brought here by his mother as an infant.

Under the actual floor of the Shrine is the Well of Spirits, which gives forth a hollow, whispering sound. Here the spirits of the departed gather twice a week, and the Shrine is surrounded by seventy thousand angels, who parade around the building, as do the pilgrims of all three faiths in emulation – on eternal guard.

Eight flights of stairs lead to the esplanade, beyond a beautiful portico on the plateau itself. On the Day of Judgment, says a tradition, the scales which will weigh human actions will be supported upon the Rock.

You can always tell a visitor who is entering the Dome for the first time, a guardian told me. As he enters, its breathtaking beauty invariably hits him with an almost physical force. Shafts of sunlight, dyed red, blue, green by the stained glass of the windows, strike straight into the half-lighted interior. In passing, these rays make the gorgeous gold inlay work of the Dome's 180-foot interior glitter. All around the walls are magnificent arabesque inscriptions, recording in Arabic the rebuilding and the name of the Defender of Islam: Sultan Saladin, Coeur de Lion's chivalrous foe in the Crusades.

Under here lies the ark of Noah, riding upon unfathomed waters...

No fewer than ninety acres comprise the total area of the Sanctuary. Within this circumference, close to the Dome itself, stands the revered Mosque of Aksa: the "Furthest Mosque." We are told that when Muhammad was carried by the magical steed Buraq on his heavenly flight, the horse alighted here, so that the Prophet could say his prayers. The Saddle of Buraq is represented by a number of marble fragments, and many other relics of varying degrees of credence are also shown.

You can see the footprint of the Prophet Edris (Enoch), the resting-place of the murderers of Thomas à Becket, Solomon's Stables, and the place of the Nineteen Nails.

These nails are said to have been hammered into rock by the Prophet Muhammad. One by one, so runs the legend, they drop through the rock. When the last one falls, it will be the end of the world. Today three nails remain, after thirteen hundred years.

The Aksa Mosque is supposed originally to have been a basilica erected by Justinian in 536, honoring the Blessed Virgin. Sultan Saladin restored the interior, marking it with his date of 1186.

Muslims and Christians alike who make the journey here are generally styled by pious local Arabs by the title of *Haj* – the honorific more usually reserved for those who make the pilgrimage to Mecca.

Back to the bustling, modern streets of the Jordan capital, and Amman seems almost like another world. There undoubtedly is a reluctance to leave Jerusalem, but at the same time everyone who goes there brings something of the atmosphere of the place back in his heart. Call it experience, or superstition, or imagination. Whatever it is, you cannot buy, sell or recreate it. Like the experience of the pilgrimage to Mecca, it stays with you for ever after that.

In lasting, deeply contemplative mood I journeyed northward, seeking a famed center of mystical thought and practice. In Syria is located one of the many Sufi monasteries, associated with the mysticism of Islam: and with hospitality and initiation, with learning and – nowadays – even powerful political penetration.

CHAPTER XXI

In Search of Venus

THE CULT OF beauty has perhaps never numbered among its devotees as many as it does today. Venus, today as four thousand years ago, symbolizes perfect womanhood the world over. Yet her true history for centuries remained one of history's profoundest enigmas: even today the whole story has not been unfolded. I went to her reputed birthplace – Cyprus – to probe the origins and reality behind the worship of the greatest goddess of Classical times. Her worship and what lies behind it provide a remarkable instance of a truth that we are only rediscovering today. Much has been written, in the purely historical sense, recording the later accretions surrounding Venus-worship. The original spirit which moved the Phoenicians to make this legendary figure their paramount deity certainly included beauty, but it went far deeper than that.

Who was Venus? Was she "born in the driven sea-foam" of the Mediterranean: or was she born at all?

Three thousand years ago, on the western coast of Cyprus – just off the coast of Asia Minor – flourished the greatest shrine of all the Classical gods. This was the mighty kingdom of Paphos, ruled by Hellenic priest-kings, tending the sacred Temple of Aphrodite, the "foam-born one."

According to Homer's *Iliad*, she was the daughter of Zeus and Dione, queen of the heavens, patroness of family life. Pious pilgrims journeyed here from all the Middle Eastern lands: from ancient Egypt, the Greek islands – from Greece itself – and the Levant. All brought gifts to the sacred grove: soldiers sought victory in battle, merchants prayed to her for success in commerce, estranged lovers addressed to Aphrodite their prayers for reconciliation.

Several thousand years before Christ, the mighty seafaring Phoenician race had migrated to Assyria from South Arabia. Their tribal system, under the guidance of energetic and capable women, was entirely matriarchal. With them to their new country they brought the goddess Ashtorath, sometimes called Ishtar. To them, this woman-deity represented much. She was the embodiment of the womanly virtues; nurtured their clan as a mother tends her child. As the goddess of maternity, the Phoenicians spoke of her as always carrying her son Tammuz within one arm, blessing him with the other. Yet, like the stern female warriors of their people, she protected their soldiers in war. Later, when they took to the sea, Ashtorath extended her benediction, in their mythology, over the oceangoing fleets that sailed as far as Cornwall and Carthage.

This was the figure – from whom the name Esther is derived – who was carried by the Phoenician traders, when they colonized Cyprus. In their legends, she was said to have been born from foam, by the sea. When they reached the strangely beautiful Paphos cliffs, topped with sylvan glades, they felt that here was a place worthy of the central shrine of their great goddess. On the hills, the summer heat is always tempered by soft breezes; the beaches are indeed washed by a strange milk-white foam. In such a place it needed little imagination to believe that a goddess might be born.

Ktima, then, as it was called, became the sacred sanctuary of the motherhood goddess. Her fame as an oracle spread throughout the known world of those times. The Greeks themselves admitted her to their mythology. After her miraculous birth in the foam, they said, she ascended to the heights of Mount Olympus, there to become one of the Twelve Olympian deities.

Standing there looking down at the strange snow-white foam in the curving bay of Ktima, one senses anew what must have been the feeling of awe that gave rise to this remarkable legend. It is not known for certain what causes the foam: certainly I have never seen its like. The possibility is, however, that some chemical element is present on the seashore, mixed with the salty water. There is something almost eerie about it all.

The Romans, when they came in contact with Aphrodite, were rapidly converted to her cult. Renaming her Venus, they were not slow to claim her as the mother of the Roman race, through her son Aeneas. Disciples of Venus among the Romans carried her worship to the British Isles; one of her temples in this country was at Stowe, another at Corbridge in Northumberland. The mailed Venus is said to be identical with the figure of Britannia which appears on the reverse of every penny. At all events Aphrodite, like Britannia, was believed to rule the waves for the Phoenician men-of-war.

One of the strangest things about Venus, however, is the development of her representation as a female figure, from her original form. For at first she was nothing but a lump of grey-black stone.

It seems that at the beginning of her worship she was regarded as the paramount deity. As such, the Phoenicians were afraid to make any figure to portray her; for, they thought, such an attempt would be bound to fail. Thus they took the black stone as a symbol, placing it in the great temple sanctuary of Paphos. Tacitus, the ancient writer, himself seems to have feared her reputed wrath when he guardedly tells his readers that the Venus of the Shrine "hath no human form."

Until relatively recently, it was not generally known that the ancient Venus was, in fact, this conical stone. One ancient coin of Bylbus, however, gives a stylized representation of the stone in its place. From this and other evidence, plus exploration on the spot, I have been able to reconstruct the main features of the shrine.

Kouklia, where the remains of the temple lie, is today a vast area of ruins. Earthquakes, Persian, Turkish and Arab conquests and civil war have all contributed to the general desolation of what must once have been a most imposing sight. Situated on a height overlooking the plain which runs down to the Mediterranean, it is one of the most charming spots on the Enchanted Isle. Still running some ten miles westward to the sea is the ancient pilgrim-way, along which millions of worshippers have poured to the temple whose mysteries were famed throughout the Classical age. Nowadays, a new road exactly follows this once-hallowed track to Ktima, fortress of the priest-kings and the world's greatest pilgrim port of former times. Most of the pilgrims traveled by this route; others, hailing from the east, disembarked at Salamis, on the Island's other side.

Within an enormous court or enclosure stood a roofed shrine, with colonnades surrounding it. Above the twin pillars of the "holy of holies" were placed sculpted doves. The stone itself stood in the center, always draped in costly coverings. Immediately facing this was the Venus altar, upon which incense burned incessantly. Legend says that, although this was always here, even the heaviest rain did not affect its burning.

Upon approaching this jealously guarded holy place, the pilgrim was expected to adhere strictly to the rituals laid down by the priest-king, and enforced by the priestesses.

At the time of the Trojan Wars the great ruler of the kingdom of Paphos, and priest of the sanctuary, was named

Kinyras; his dynasty ruled the country and the temple for over a thousand years. It is he who was said to have introduced the famous mysteries of ancient Egypt to the shrine, and to have practiced alchemy there.

There were three degrees of these "mysteries," performed by selected pilgrims. The first took three days. On the first day, they participated in games; on the second, they bathed in the sea in tribute to Venus; on the last occasion, bloodless sacrifices were offered to the goddess, in honor of the greatness of motherhood. Women, particularly, prayed for beauty for themselves and for their children's success.

The highest degree, to which only a few were initiated, was known as the Mystery of Aphrodite and Adonis, her lover. Very little is known about this ritual, except that it emphasized the abiding beauty of love.

Those who were permitted to touch the stone itself were presented with a symbol and a piece of salt. These emblems, in return for which a coin was offered, were held to be lucky charms. In the case of soldiers, they brought victory in battle; for others, they ensured the achievement of the devotee's wish.

There are many mysteries of Venus still to be solved. Where, for instance, is the once-famed sarcophagus of jasper stone, which once decorated the shrine? Until the time of the Turks it was kept in the Cathedral of Saint Sophia, in the capital, Nicosia. Some hundred years ago it disappeared. The local legend in connection with this is that it fell from the skies as a bed for Aphrodite. Others held that it was created by the gods in an attempt to make an image of her. At all events, this colossal block of jasper has completely disappeared.

At another spot is the reputed Tomb of Venus. This forms another clue to the rites of Paphos, for there are several references to the fact that the goddess "used periodically to die." This event did not take place regularly, as in the case of sun-worship cults, when the sun is believed to die in winter. This, together with an increasing use of a human figure to represent the goddess, may mean another thing. There is a distinct possibility that from time to time young women were chosen to embody the attributes of Venus as a deity of love. In such cases, of course, they would die one day. Their bodies – as semi-divine creatures – might then be buried in a place of special distinction. Plausibility is lent to this by the fact that there are several reputed tombs of Venus in Cyprus.

Nowadays, the black stone itself reposes in Nicosia Museum. Deep indentations upon it show where the priests used to anoint the surface in honor of their goddess. The entire surface of the cone has been worn smooth by generations of pilgrim hands. On the Temple site, immense mounds of rubble, marble columns and walls lie strewn over a great area. Secret passages on the neglected ground, apparently leading nowhere, probably mark the entrances to the chambers of the priests.

But the worship of Venus still goes on. While in Cyprus, I was intrigued by reports that villagers still secretly anoint stones in her name. One friend took me to several places where, at nightfall, young girls in groups of three and four at a time, entered the temple precincts.

Each, with a little pot of water and a small oil-soaked rag, went to an upstanding stone to make her wish at Aphrodite's temple.

Venus has again recently begun to arouse the interest of archaeologists; some digging in the temple site has recently been undertaken – but little fresh light has been thrown upon the heyday of Aphrodite-worship. Piecing together the story of Venus from the Black Stone of the Phoenicians to the Venus de Milo of perfect womanhood was a fascinating study and adventure.

My own impression is that it is unlikely that tracing the origins of the cult beyond the Phoenicians will be possible – if it can ever be done – without extensive research in Asia Minor – and possibly even South Arabia, where the first settlements were.

Turning from the remote past to the trail of the everyday present, I followed up the next important event in the lives of those charming village girls, whom I saw anointing large and small stones with rose-oil as they ask that they should be blessed with a good husband, for among the mixed population the village folk – Greeks and Turks alike – delight in their traditional wedding ceremonies, and the emphasis upon married bliss.

As in every land where heavy modern industries are few, peasant life in Cyprus retains color and delight: but here, perhaps more than any other place, the rich history of Crusaders, Saracens, Pharaohs and Venetians seems to give an ideal background to life's enjoyment.

Nine out of ten Cypriots live in their picturesque mountain or lowland villages. Whether in the upland vineyards, among the oranges of the western shores, or among shepherd communities of the pine-clad Mount Olympus ("Home of the Gods"), weddings are a most important affair.

Before the actual ceremony, negotiations spread over months of discussion between the parents of the betrothed. Over Turkish coffee and sugarplums, the two fathers sit discussing the bridal dowry: how much the girl is to bring, what the husband-to-be agrees to do for her, and all the more matter-of-fact sides of the case.

For the women, this is a time of planning, excitement and hard work. Friends, relations and well-wishers are pressed into unrelenting service to prepare lavishly embroidered blouses, wide peasant skirts, all the trousseau that every self-respecting heiress of Venus must have.

The mothers of the bride and groom alike are in perpetual conclave to decide the plan of the house, and its furnishing. These are supplied by the parents of the bride.

As soon as all is arranged, rings are exchanged by the pair: this means that the ceremony may take place at any time. For days before the appointed date, willing hands slave at the bride's house preparing vast quantities of food which will be eaten by the guests. As the guests will include the whole village – and sometimes the next one as well – this is no light task.

The volunteers bring bottles of wine, fruit preserved in syrup, bake cakes, make macaroni and a hundred other dishes of the country. Ten "best men" and the same number of bridesmaids are selected among great scenes of competition. As in the West, it is considered lucky to be one of these.

Gaily embroidered clothes and silken pieces are meanwhile being made by the best needlewomen of the community. As they work, traditional songs are sung, and a violinist plays over them, to ensure good luck for the happy couple.

At last all is prepared for the ceremony. Guests pour into the village hall, or the largest rooms of the farm house. As each arrives she is welcomed, and rosewater dropped on her palm by the bride's mother. On these occasions the bridesmaids wear wide peasant skirts, and a sort of jacket somewhat in the Balkan and Turkish style. Wide-sleeved, of velvet, this waistcoat is tightly caught at the waist, while its front is open and faced with the famed lace of Lefkara. A jaunty headdress in piratical style completes the costume.

Then come the dances. Wearing flat-heeled shoes – but nowadays sometimes Western ones – the women link hands and keep time to the lively music, played by a band of violinists. At the end of the tune the right arm is raised in a dramatic gesture by the dancers, and everyone cheers. There are two dances: the first out in the open, the other inside the house, beside the bridal bed.

As the church bells begin to peal, a huge procession wends its way toward the scene of the ceremony. Before the marriage starts, the priest hands out candles. Each guest lights his, and these are held in the hand until all is over.

One of the lighter aspects of the marriage is when the priest comes to the words "To love and obey." As soon as this phrase has been pronounced, the groom treads on the bride's toes, to make sure she takes good note of it!

Then back to the feast. At the bride's house, cakes and every manner of good things are laid before all and sundry. Quantities of the local sweet – not very potent – wine are quaffed. The newlyweds share a pair of roasted doves, to cement their symbolic happiness.

The wedding may be over, but the celebrations are not.

For at least three more days the dancing, bonfires, fiddling and singing will continue – mostly at the bride's expense. The main course offered at these banquets is called *Resi*. Made of wheat and lamb, it must be prepared with great ceremony. Girls, singing traditional songs, take turns at grinding the flour, which has been inspected and blessed with considerable gravity weeks before, and carefully locked up "so that no evil may befall it."

A specially made bed, in whose preparation every woman of the village has taken part, is the gift of the community to the couple. Amid complicated songs and dances, the mattress is made with meticulous care. Aromatic herbs and silver coins for good luck are sewn into one corner. Every little detail of a Cyprus village wedding has its own ceremony, dress and song.

While there is no going away on a honeymoon, there is such a burst of jollification and revelry during this entire period of several weeks that it more than compensates for it, as far as the people of Cyprus are concerned.

It is refreshing to feel that there are still many who can get so much fun out of their traditional folk-life: and who show not the slightest sign of wanting modernity in what is an extremely contented existence.

CHAPTER XXII

Sorcerer's Apprentice

EVERYONE HAS HEARD of Yoga; people are prepared to believe that Tibetan divines can sit for weeks stark naked in the snow, and derive some spiritual advantage therefrom: or, at least, suffer no lasting harm from the experience. The witchcraft of Africa is an established fact. But how many people in the West know anything much about Sufism?

The mystical philosophy of the Muslims is one of those things which is an open secret to the people of the East, yet as impenetrable to a Westerner as anything you can imagine. It is practiced by perhaps ten to twenty million people. In some places, such as Muslim India or Afghanistan, almost every adult male is affiliated to a greater or lesser degree to one of the four main Orders. True, there are books on the subject in English; certain Western Orientalists (ridiculous term) have even made a special study of it. Some of the East's greatest literature has been written by Sufi mystics, and this has formed the source of material for the plausible but useless books "explaining" Islamic mysticism to the West.

Writing, as I do, in English, and for a Western public, I can understand some of the problems that orientalists have to face in trying to describe something for which there are no precise parallels in European thought. It is easy to simplify, easy to get a general idea of Sufism, possible to put down on paper general remarks which seem to have authority, but merely scratch the surface. This is the temptation to which too many of the otherwise highly respected professors of oriental studies have succumbed. For I would rather go on record as saying that these sages understand more than they write but find it hard to write it, than to hold that they understand it not at all.

Perhaps the difficulty can in part be likened to the task of an outsider studying freemasonry. Those who want to go further into Sufism will have to seek elsewhere than in these pages for a deep presentation of the cult.[5] All that I can hope to do here is to give a general outline of some of the main features of the system and then plunge into my story: for this, after all, is a travel book, even if it does not dwell upon every moment of my journeyings, and deals with my search for the unusual, and the highlights of what I actually saw and heard in the Middle East.

Sufism is organized mainly into four schools, or semi-monastic Orders, each deriving from a Teacher who developed a rigidly organized system of recitations, exercises and studies. The object of this effort is the refinement of the soul, and the unification of the mind of man with that of God. Sufism is Islamic, and for that reason it is held to be impossible for a non-Muslim to become a Sufi. A staggering number of miracles are attributed to Sufis, including foreknowledge, levitation, power over trees, plants and other natural things, curing of disease, flying from one place to another – and supernatural power in most of its aspects.

Time as we know it is of little interest to Sufis. They claim to be in contact telepathically with one another irrespective of time and distance. Long-dead saints are believed to be in active contact with living divines. These are the people

---

[5] Details are given in my *Oriental Magic*.

known as Dervishes in Turkey and elsewhere, and many of those who have the name of *fakir* (i.e. "humble") in India. A son generally joins the *Halqa* (circle) to which his father belonged. There is no celibacy in Sufism, and no set time for the transition between one stage of power and the next. All depends upon individual progress. The Sufis, incidentally, do not believe in reincarnation, but rather in the unreality of death.

Now Sufis do not preach the cult. It is up to the inquiring youth – for such he generally is – to seek out a Sufi circle and apply for admission. No fees are charged, and once a candidate is accepted, he is under an absolute vow of obedience stricter than any military code that I know. The purpose of the development of the Sufi himself is to become a perfect man, and hence to be of the greatest possible value to the community.

I had been present often enough at the gatherings of Sufis in various places, taken part in their recitations and listened to their discourses. Now, in Syria, I decided to see whether I could penetrate further into the actual active side of Sufi life. I wanted to get a clearer, firsthand view of the whole thing.

At Yeniburj (whose locating was difficult, since its very existence was denied by some) I made my way up the steep slope of the hillside, where the ancient monastery – a collection of weathered former fortifications – stood out against the late afternoon sky. I had a letter to the *Wali* (saint) of the place, whom I shall call Sheikh Ibrahim. The "lay brethren" whom I passed on the incline were pious-looking men, wearing the patched cloak of the dervish, carrying water, tending vegetable gardens, milking goats. I was taken into the largest building to await the arrival of the Sheikh.

This community, it seemed, was composed mainly of refugees from the Kemalist regime in Turkey, where the

Republic had dissolved the monasteries in the 1920s, and the practice of Sufism became illegal.

Filtering southward into Syria, these Sufis had taken up their abode in the ruined fortress, added a number of smaller buildings to it, and now carried on the cult free of any interference.

The hall of the castle where I sat was high, arched and surrounded with cloisters, after the fashion of the Middle Eastern caravansary. In one corner of the huge courtyard food was being cooked over a brazier. A Sufi cook turned *shashlik* meat on a skewer over the sullen flames, and watched a soup cauldron simmering over a slow, sullen charcoal fire. Ranged beside him were the communal soup-bowls of the community: for nobody is allowed to have private property, and there is one famous (probably apocryphal) story of a venerable Sufi being "drummed out of the Order" for having indicated a preference for one bowl over the others.

The corner of the courtyard facing Mecca was decorated by a painted niche, with the word Allah written upon it. I was seated on one of the rugs which were arranged in horseshoe form around the southern part of the arena. From the fort itself came the monotonous rhythm of the *halqa* in action: there must have been some three hundred voices intoning the chant: *La-illaha-illa-lah!* (no God but Allah), and I could imagine the circle of worshippers swaying backward and forward to the beat of the syllables. This is a familiar Sufi exercise (*dhikr*) in all Muslim countries.

A young member of the Order, dressed in a cotton mantle of subdued Sufi orange, brought me a copy of the Qur'an, and I immersed myself in reading it. Suddenly, from the very top of the castle's tower, the long-drawn-out, thin and appealing cry of the Muezzin echoed forth: "*Hayya alaessalah...*" ("Come to Prayer, Come to Success!"). It was time for the afternoon devotions, for Sufi exercises are additional to the five obligatory prayers of established Islam.

I hurried to the fountain in the middle of the courtyard, and performed my ablutions: washing hands, arms, face and feet. As I looked round, the whole place seemed suddenly full of hurrying figures, heading for the interior of the fort. I followed them into the Mosque. This, in the very center of the building, was an enormous chamber without windows; bare except for matting on the floor and the names of the Prophet and the Four Caliphs inscribed upon medallions high upon the walls.

After the congregational prayers were over, and we sat silent for a few minutes in private contemplation, I looked around to get some idea of my companions. They were a very assorted-looking lot. About half of the five-hundred-odd were dressed in long orange robes. Others wore cotton garments covered with patches: both varieties of Sufi "uniform." Each one had hair reaching to his shoulders, and most had beards. There was something very monkish about them. They seemed to come in all sizes, and ranged in age from perhaps about twenty to the Sheikh himself, who could have been a hundred, with his white hair and staff. There was not much light, for the oil lamps were low and flickering.

I presented myself to the Sheikh. He was tall, thin and serious of face. "Welcome, brother, stay as long as you will..."

Slowly, in twos and threes, the congregation broke up. I was told that for the purposes of study, the community was divided into sections, each under a leader. Between the hours of prayer, each leader took his section into one or other of the rooms set aside for their use, and gave them instruction. At certain times the whole community assembled in the Zawiya (assembly-hall) and carried out physical and religious exercises under the guidance of the Sheikh or one of his five assistants. These assistant sheikhs were the most developed spiritually after the Sheikh, and one day one of them would take over the saffron robe of leadership of the monastery, while the others would go out into the world to form their own communities.

We returned to the courtyard where the *Diwan* of the Sheikh was assembling. Each Sufi has his own rug or mat, and his own position in the horseshoe. These are factors which are determined by the Sheikh, and none may occupy another's seat. The arrangement of the places denotes the degree of spiritual enlightenment which the individual has attained.

Because my Persian was better than my Syrian Arabic, and possibly due to the fact that Persian is a classical tongue of Sufism, the Sheikh and his "cabinet" carried out their deliberations in that language. Their linguistic ability was considerable. The session was divided into three parts. First came secular matters. One by one, the lay brethren in charge of various activities came and presented accounts and reports. The Sheikh adjudicated upon small matters, and gave general administrative instructions.

Then the uninitiated were dismissed, and the Sheikh gave an interpretation of one of the works of Al-Ghazzali. For over an hour he held forth on the meaning of one passage of the *Renaissance of Religious Sciences*, while the assembly sat mute and relaxed, allowing every word to sink in. There was no doubt that he was a man of the most profound knowledge. Speaking without a note, and without even the text before him, he interpreted an obscure part of the most difficult work of Islamics, with profuse literal quotations from the Qur'an, which he knew by heart.

Up to this point silence had been obligatory upon all. No questions might be asked.

Now, however, came the debate. One of the Sufis had challenged another to a debate upon the reality of existence and the meaning of time. First one spoke, then the other. Then the first was allowed to reply. Poems and passages from classics were recited to embellish and elucidate points. A number of works of vast erudition unfamiliar to me were quoted *in extenso*. Then the others were asked as to whether anyone wished to comment upon the debate. One by one, three of the more important Sufis spoke for and against the motion, as it were.

Then silence. The Sheikh summed up the entire range of the arguments and gave his verdict, rather after the fashion of an appeal judge in England. This was probably my most absorbing experience of all during that Middle Eastern journey. This seemed standard-enough procedure here, but the range and depth of the proceedings – entirely extemporaneous – were amazing.

Now, as the evening shadows were gathering, we lined up for our food at the "kitchen" on the other side of the square. Each man was issued with a bowl filled with vegetable soup, in which pieces of roast meat had been included; a large, round unleavened loaf was added, and a bottle of water from the well. We sat round in a circle, eating – as is the custom – in complete silence. There was no order of precedence in meals, and the Sheikh sat next to a beardless youth, while I was flanked on the one side by one of the superior sages, and on the other by the cook himself.

When we had finished, and washed our hands, faces and bowls, we performed the evening prayer in congregation at the Mosque.

As I was leaving, the Sheikh took me aside and asked me whether I would join his *halqa* at their special devotions that night. Trying not to show too much delight, I agreed. He told me to be in the Mosque at midnight. I had about four hours until then, which I spent exploring the monastery. In one room three dervish tailors sat, repairing the garments of their fellows with bone needles, by the light of oil lamps. Clothes were, it seemed, communally owned. Next door was the weaving shop, where material was made from goat hair for sale locally. In the library twelve copyists sat laboriously illuminating manuscripts of the Qur'an and the Traditions of the Prophet. As each page was finished, it was checked for accuracy five times, and then passed to the Chief Librarian – an elderly Yemenite – to be finally pitted against his memory.

My guide, Abdullah, had been with the monastery only two years, before which he had been a doctor who had taken his degree in Berlin. He told me a remarkable story about the Librarian, which I give here just as I heard it.

"Last year a wandering dervish came this way, and asked if we would lend him one of the manuscripts. It was the only copy we had, and normally it would not have been lent under any circumstances. But the Sheikh agreed, because the wanderer was known for his piety and complete indifference to things of the world. It was not thought possible that he would lose it or sell it. Unfortunately we miscalculated. When he reached Damascus, the dervish met a man who he thought would benefit more by the book than he himself would. So he lent it to him. This man died on a pilgrimage to Mecca, and his effects were dispersed. Nobody knew where the book was.

"When the news came to the Librarian he simply sighed and wrote out the book from memory!"

I believe that this may be possible, because the practice of committing to memory is not uncommon, and very many children are schooled in this technique by having learned the Qur'an by heart. This takes two to four years. The Qur'an being in rhymed Arabic, the task is easier than it would otherwise be.

There were about thirty dervishes in the Mosque when I arrived just after midnight. After a few minutes the Sheikh appeared, and led us across the courtyard into a subterranean chamber about a hundred feet long and half as wide. The ceiling was low, the floor was thickly carpeted with Persian rugs, the walls were whitewashed, and quite bare. We removed our sandals at the door, where several Sufis stood as if on guard.

The congregation formed up in a circle, facing inward, seated crosslegged. I sat beside the Sheikh. For a moment all was silence.

Then the Sheikh intoned the words *Allahu!* about six times, in rapid succession. From the other side of the circle the cry was taken up. Soon every one of us was repeating the phrase (God Exists!) as fast as we could, still maintaining a rhythm. Then, slowly at first, edging into the recitation, about ten of the dervishes added the word Akbar, Akbar, *Akbar, AKBAR,* AKBAR, *AKBAR!* The phrase now ran: God Exists, Greater than All Else! As the rhythm was established, the bodies of the devotees swayed backward and forward in time to the syllables. I noticed that a few of them seemed to be more affected than the rest. Some had their eyes closed, others had a fixed, wide-eyed expression. There were small beads of perspiration appearing on every face. Then, as if in response to a signal, half of them started to clap, in monotonous time, and the shouting grew in volume, thrown back by the bare walls, seeming to reverberate through one's entire frame... Alla*ho-Ak*bar, Alla*ho-Ak*bar, Alla*hu*, Alla*hu*... Then it faded, and finally there was silence again.

I looked around me. Three of the dervishes seemed to be in trances. One lolled forward, eyes closed, head on his chest, arms clasped before him. The other two, with eyes wide open, were directly facing me, and such was the intensity of their stare that I could not face it. There was something uncanny about the whole thing. Even the room seemed to have become uncomfortably hot, though I knew that it should be cool, at this time of night, underground... I began to feel that my own senses were being affected, I thought I could see something standing beside me; a man with a beard, towering, surely far too tall for a real human being? He wore long robes, and had a staff – no, a snake – or something, in his hand.

I was shaken out of my reverie by a touch on the arm by the Sheikh. He beckoned me closer, and I turned toward him. Into my ear he said: "Remember this: you are going to be a big man, an important man. I see you walking about in a large garden, there are roses, and there are tulips. You are going into a huge palace, there is a red carpet on the steps, you are asking for something, and it will be granted..."

He stopped, his voice becoming so slow that it sounded almost funny. I whispered in his ear: "You are speaking of the past, Great Sheikh, these things have happened. I am a poor man now, and probably will remain so. I have no hopes of being great or powerful."

The Sheikh had described, in a rather garbled form, things which had happened to me. He spoke again. "I make no mistake, they may have happened, but they did not happen like that. Your life is a set pattern, and I want you to know that this pattern will come round again, but slightly different. Here is a watchword: 'Build to the Sea!'"

"I do not understand you."

"Never mind. Stop thinking. There is fear in your heart. Nothing is going to happen to you. Why should you worry?"

I still do not know what Build to the Sea means; or whether the Sheikh snatched some images from my memory and retold them to me – or if so, why... This is in any case not the main point of the story.

I decided just to let the whole thing roll over me, as it were, and sort out impressions the following day. I knew that Sufis are not dangerous, and anyway I had little to lose.

Suddenly, one of the dervishes stood bolt upright and shouted something which I did not understand. Immediately he was followed by three more, and then another. Together they drew apart from the rest, and started to whirl counter clockwise at first slowly, then faster and faster. These were the actual Dancing Dervishes – of the Bektashi Order – in action!

I would have given anything to have had my camera with me. This thought brought me fully alert again. I decided to think of secular things, to clear the brain. I thought of the smoky lighting. Not much good, even for a fast lens and hypersensitized film. At that speed of movement, too, it would have been impossible to get a picture without flash. Flash would not be allowed...

Then, as if he had been struck by a heavy blow from behind, the tallest of the whirling dervishes collapsed in a heap on the ground. Then the one next to him, then a third. They rolled over where they lay, eyes open, glazed, faces turned toward the ceiling. The other two continued their dance. This time they were circling one another, repeating Hy Hy, H, H, Hu Hu, Hy, ALLAH, at the tops of their voices, with arms outstretched like so many birds in mime. None of them seemed to go into a trance. After a few more circles, they came and sat down quietly outside our squatting circle.

Then another, who had been sitting quietly passing the beads of a rosary through his fingers, gave an unearthly shriek, and fell forward flat on his face. Gently, the Sheikh turned him over. His eyes were shut, and his breathing was so shallow that it was imperceptible to me.

We sat for what seemed only a few minutes more, when the door opened and one of the brethren called the summons to the Dawn Prayer. The session had lasted all night.

The recumbent figures came alive at this. All the Sufis then shook hands and greeted each other with salaams, as if they had been separated for some time. It was at this time that I felt an almost overwhelming urge to stay at the monastery, and to take part in their ceremonies.

The Sheikh knew it, for when he took my hand he said: "Your time is not yet. You have places to see and people to meet. Remember what I have told you."

I asked him, later, about the state of the dervishes whom I had seen in a trance. He told me that according to their belief they were in a state of nearness to the Supreme Power, and that in order to commune with it this state of ecstasy required that all connection with the physical body should cease: a sort of short-circuiting of the nervous system.

I told him that I had seen such things in hypnosis and also in mediumistic trance. "Yes, I know about these things. They are called *ruhaniyyat*, and are against Islam. Our trance is different, and each time the person achieves it he becomes more powerful in the spiritual sense. You cannot say the same for *ruhaniyyat*.

"You must remember," he went on, "that our exercises have little to do with ordinary, mundane magic. In a sense we are cultivators of a divine form of magic. But the normal and worldly magic is to be found elsewhere. If you want to see that, why not amuse yourself by visiting Musa the Jew who lives in Damascus?"

I asked him whether he did not think that magic of that kind was dangerous or deceptive, or perhaps diabolical?

"Everything is bad in accordance with the use to which it is put. Sufism cannot be put to evil uses, simply because its power comes from God. Mundane magic can be put to evil or good uses, just as any other non-spiritual thing can be put to such uses. If you want to achieve an evil end by magic, you can, and if you want to accomplish good, you can

Top left: King Zahir Shah of Afghanistan (arms half-raised in prayer) beside the silver-set Black Stone in the Kaaba

Top right: Cloisters of the Great Mosque, Mecca

Bottom left: Inside the Tomb: Original banner of the Mahdi. Bottom line reads: 'Muhammad the Mahdi, Deputy of the Messenger of Allah'

Bottom right: The Kaaba in the center of the Great Mosque

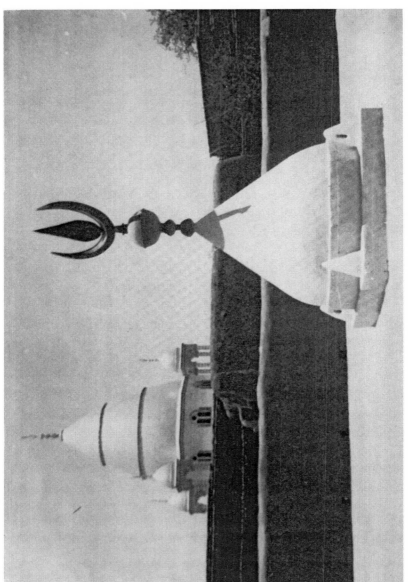

Foreground: former cupola of the Mahdi's Tomb.   *Background*: new Tomb of the Mahdi

do so. What you do not understand is that you do not yet understand – except very approximately – what is evil and what is good. That is why it is best to stick to Sufism, which is entirely and essentially good."

And now as to how I became a sorcerer's apprentice.

I traveled down from Yeniburj to Damascus without having any precise plans for bearding Musa in his den, but thought that he might care to give me some ideas on magic if I showed interest.

And so it turned out. Musa (Moses) the Jew lived in a small house not far from the Great Bazaar in Damascus, and still does, as far as I know.

I found him by merely asking everyone I met in the street if he knew Musa the Jew. Now many people did know him, and after about an hour I was directed to the clay-built whitewashed dwelling, leaning up against a high wall, where the master was to be found. I knocked on the black wood door. No answer, no sign of life. A hideous dog with one eye slipped down the street and shied away from me. I looked around. An eye was visible, peeping from the first-floor window. Then it became a head. It was a woman whom I took for a Jewess, and risked my only Hebrew word in this very Arab territory: "*Shalom!*" The face disappeared, shuffling feet. The door was unbolted. An aged crone stood before me, mouthing words in a soft uncheerful-sounding tongue.

Musa Ejfendi fi? She took me into a small room, neatly furnished in Arabian urban style. Divans ran the length of the walls, rugs of Armenian origin on the floor, a couple of small Indian tables with brass tops held a water-pipe and a dusty manuscript. I sat down and waited.

Musa the Jew, stroking his long grey beard and dressed in a flowing blue robe, came into the room. He smiled, his creased face and blue eyes giving a strange effect of half-pleasure, half-caution. He certainly did not exactly correspond with my idea of what he might be like. The black skullcap was there, the robe, the patriarchal beard. But the size of the man! He must have been well over six feet tall, and broad. His hands were large, and on his right thumb there glittered a red-stoned silvery ring.

He came up to me and, before I could rise, took my hands in his, then sat beside me on the divan. A small boy appeared with coffee on a tray, and we drank the first sip in silence.

"I am Musa, son of Yusif," he spoke in heavily accented Arabic. I had the idea that he might have been some sort of central European, from his speech.

"I have been told that you are the master of unusual sciences, and as a traveler and seeker after knowledge came to salute you, O Sage."

"You are not an Arab?"

"No, I am a traveler" – the term that is used in these parts by someone who does not wish to identify himself with any particular country or people.

"Muslim?"

"Yes."

"How did you hear of me?"

"From Sheikh Ibrahim, Saint of the Bektashi."

"And from anyone else?"

"From the many with whom I have spoken, among whom your knowledge and piety are legend."

He smiled. "From Sheikh Ibrahim, you mean. Well, he is a good man, though somewhat narrow. Islam considers that everything that came before was superseded by itself. Is that not so?"

"Anything you say, O Sage."

"Well, if you want to see something of interest, I can show you things that will surprise you. But I want you to know that you must become my assistant for the purposes of these experiments. This will mean that you must not teach any of the arts to anyone who is not fit to know them, and you must also promise that you will not exercise the Art except when you are convinced that in so doing you will be in harmony with the destiny of people and of the world."

"I am afraid that I am not at any stage which would enable me to determine such things."

"That is so much to the good. Regard these experiences, then, as merely for your own education. When people come to me it is generally to achieve something for them, or to take them as students. I do not do either, in most cases."

Musa led me to an even smaller room, where colored tiles formed the floor and walls. In the middle a fountain played. "Here you will bathe yourself completely, understand? When you are ceremonially clean, put on the white robes and sandals that the boy will bring you. Then enter the room opposite, and do not before. If you want anything, clap your hands."

I was not at all sure as to what I had got myself into, but decided to go through with it.

Half an hour later I was ready. On my feet were a pair of new white sandals. The robe consisted of a long cotton garment, with wide sleeves, and three or four signs embroidered on the breast. A white skullcap was also included, so I put this on.

With some apprehension I edged open the door of the magician's parlor. He was seated at a large table, surrounded by a bewildering array of what was probably alchemical apparatus: test tubes in bank after bank of racks, retorts, crucibles, stills of flameproof glass, bottles containing red, white and green liquids. As the door opened he waved me to a seat at the same table.

On the black surface of the table was a large book, bound in vellum, with characters inscribed on its pages. The Sage was turning the leaves with a look of intense preoccupation.

I looked further round the room. It was oblong, and we were sitting in a narrow part about one-third of the length, which was divided from the rest by a white line. The remaining portion of the floor was marked off into a large square. Within this, concentric with the square, was embedded a double circle in iron.

Inside the circle were inscribed signs and Hebrew words. Standing in the circle were such things as a brazier, filled with burning charcoal, two candles in sticks, a vessel containing water, a manuscript and a high table or altar.

"Are you ready?" Musa took a long, bared sword in his hand, and took me by the arm, muttering as we entered the circle. He made me stand on a spot marked with a star design, and told me that if I moved from that point, no matter what happened, I might die. "So stand still."

I didn't believe it, but I stood still just the same. That sword did not look too reassuring.

There was a crackle and flash as Musa threw some powder on the fire. A sweet, heavy odor began to rise from it. He handed me a book. "Read this."

"I cannot, it is in Hebrew."

With an impatient gesture, he snatched the book, and intoned: "AGLA, ADONAE, JEHOVA," and many more words. After he spoke each name, more incense was put on the brazier. The room began to feel oppressively hot, in spite of the fact that I was wearing only the thin cotton mantle. I began to think of the same sort of atmosphere up at Yeniburj.

Another flash of fire, as the magician plunged his blade right into the fire, with a fierce, almost furious movement. From the breast of his white robe he took a piece of paper with a five-pointed star drawn on it, and intoned a number of sentences in a hostile and heavy voice.

Then the whole thing started all over again. I was getting a little tired, and wondered when it would all end. Suddenly, through the smoke of the incense, Musa pointed with a white, metal-bound stick to the opposite wall. Something seemed to be moving. As I watched I saw that it was a picture, rather like a three-dimensional color film. It was a scene – a picture of Cairo, as if taken from a stationary airplane hovering above the city. It did not move from side to side like an ordinary movie, but just grew larger, as if we were swooping down from an immense height. Soon I could see figures in the streets, crowds, trams, cars, even peanut-sellers. It was a scene I knew well, though never from this angle...

Then the angle changed. We were over Roda Island now, and moving toward a house, set in palm trees on the island itself.

The camera seemed to alight on the roof, and then moved with incredible rapidity to a scene within the house. This was a large, airy room. About twelve men were seated round a long table. They were dressed in the blue robe and red turban of Azhar University. Before each one was a notepad, ink and some sort of agenda.

We – or the camera, or whatever it was – hovered over the table. One man was talking, and the others sat listening. I could hear no sound, but the man's lips were moving, as if in emphatic speech. "What is he saying?" I spoke to Musa, who was dropping more incense on the fire.

"I hear him, you cannot. Silence, this is important..."

Suddenly, as I leant forward, my head projecting beyond the precincts of the circle, the picture snapped out. Musa turned to me with his face working. "Fool, idiot, son of a devil! What have you done! You have ruined everything! It has gone away!"

He dragged me back into the circle. I am afraid that I was cowering a little by this time. I did not believe that the apparition was anything more than a film show, designed to impress the credulous, but I had not bargained for the fury of the magician.

I stood in silence while the conjurations and incense-casting, the exhibiting of the star and the plunging of the sword into the fire, went on, with Musa seemingly getting more and more worked up all the time. But nothing happened. Finally Musa took me by the hand and led me out of the circle.

I was feeling very foolish, quite upset and at a loss. But Musa seemed to have regained his temper. "I have something in this book" – indicating the tome that he had been reading when I entered the room – "which I have wanted for some time. I think your coming was most fortunate. Change your clothes now, and go. If you need money, I will give you a little. You have helped me. I am sorry that I spoke harshly to you."

When I had dressed I went into the small reception room again. Musa was waiting for me.

"Now, say that all is forgotten?"

"Yes, but will you not show me something more?" I wanted to gather more material, and now I felt better, though I still could not understand what his object was.

"No, you must go now, it is best. If you stay here you may not be safe."

I went out into the darkness and back to my hotel without being able to fathom the experience at all. It was like something snatched out of sequence from a novel; like a half-dream.

Normal thinking could not account for it. If Musa was really able to conjure up pictures of places hundreds of miles away, what was the purpose of it? If he was tricking me, why? I did not give him anything for it. In fact, he offered me money. The only other solution was that he was mad, or merely indulged a warped desire to impress others. If that was really the case, he had certainly gone to some expense to get most unusual three-dimensional movie-pictures of Cairo in full color – and he would have needed a helicopter to obtain such static high-altitude photographs. Perhaps you can think of something to explain all this? It is easy to dismiss such things as hallucination: but not so easy when you are the person to whom they have happened.

...My Arab-African itinerary was complete. Now, in stimulating contrast, for what was a pilgrimage of a different kind. Giving uneasy Pakistan but a cursory glance, I hastened northwest toward my native Afghan glens: to the land of tough warriors, pomegranates, fat-tailed sheep, lapis lazuli and – perhaps, who knew – the first photograph of the Afridi Chief Ipi, terror of the ranges...

CHAPTER XXIII

Guerrilla King of No Man's Land

IT WAS INDEPENDENCE Day in Kabul. For the past week swashbuckling clan chiefs from every part of Afghanistan had been swaggering through the decorated bazaars, killing time between one gigantic feast and the next, watching the rough-and-tumble of the fierce "rugby on horseback" which is called *Buz-Kashi* and played with up to a hundred a side.

The mountain kingdom's capital echoed to the passing and repassing of gun-carriages, jackbooted *élite* guards, wild horsemen from the North, cheers for the dashing young king Muhammad Zahir Shah.

At night throughout the three-day celebrations – stretched by popular demand unofficially to nearer ten – fireworks and floodlighting of the Royal Palace provided a real treat for mountain warriors, fleece-coated Uzbeks and dreamy-eyed nomads from far-off Turkistan.

I had been in Afghanistan just three months, seeking the Fakir of Ipi everywhere – but there seemed no trace.

I knew that he had escaped yet again from the Pakistan side of the southern borderland, that a Pathan Government had been set up somewhere in the Free Land this side of the Khyber. How to find the Fakir, even though the very streets of this city swarmed with his clansmen, his close supporters, was still a mystery.

In Pakistan, nobody knew anything about the Fakir. "Go to Kabul, he is hand-in-glove with the Afghans!"

In the Afghan capital there was friendship, cooperation, green tea and parties. There was no Fakir of Ipi. "We do not know where Ipi is. Foreign journalists have been waiting months to get a lead on him."

One man here, who had never left Kabul, spent days pencilling his Exclusive Story, on the theory that nobody had interviewed the Fakir, probably nobody ever would, and he might get away with it in some American paper.

"'*I meet the Mad Fakir*,' plenty of local color, and you're home," he told me.

There was no doubt that the average Afghan was pro-Fakir to the end. Capturing the popular imagination as the daredevil will-o"-the-wisp whom none could see, whose exploits had for thirty years rung from one end of the Frontier to the other, Ipi was certainly Hero Number One to them. But none of them had met him.

The grim-browed Pathans of the Free Land between Pakistan and Afghanistan might come to Kabul, were to be seen sauntering through the streets: of their leader they would speak not at all.

One night I was invited to a feast held in honor of a visiting Chief, Yakub Khan. Within the immense embroidered Tatar tent, Herati carpets and silk bolsters were our seats. Some three hundred people sat cross-legged around the colorful, brown and red woven tablecloths spread with costly aromatic *pilau*, golden chickens peeping shyly from the mounds of yellow-tinted rice.

Several hours and some gallons of green tea later, full and weary, I followed Yakub to the garden for the bonfire sword dance, surrounded by turbaned warriors hanging with every variety of offensive weapon that they found portable.

I was trying to keep up with the Khan's appetite for dried fruit – and his homemade jokes – when he spoke to me in the rough Pushtu of the mountains. Persian was the best I could do, Pushtu was really too much.

"You don't know Pushtu?" Not to speak. Certainly not the Waziri dialect. "How could you talk to Ipi, then?" I understood that an approach was being made.

"In Persian."

"I see. Do you know my clan?"

I told him that I knew that he was a Waziri. "Yes, but I am a Turi-Zai." This is Ipi's own branch of the Waziris.

The craggy, bearded face, topped by a carelessly tied black turban, came close to mine. "If you are a traitor, you will die, after being toasted."

This was something right out of a scriptwriter's imagination. I told the Khan that I wanted to see the Fakir, and that I had no opinion at all about him, except that I knew of his bravery in leading his supporters during twenty years of Frontier war.

"The Fakir will see you at Gruik. When Yahja Gul Jan comes, you will know the time. The country is full of spies. If you come, you must swear on your blood to tell no military information except what we allow you. You can stay three days at Gruik; you will have to spend at least a month in Kabul after you return from there. During that time, our people will watch you."

Fair enough, I thought. A lifetime of intrigue and frontier raiding had certainly taught the Fakir a thing or two about undercover work.

I was beginning to feel more than ever like an international spy. The suspense was acute. There was the fear that this was just a joke, either by someone who knew my quest, or even by the Fakir himself.

Three days passed, without any sign of Gul Jan, whoever he might be. I took long walks through mulberry gardens, along the magnificent tree-lined road to Dar-el-Aman, into the mountain valley of Paghman. Nobody seemed to be following me.

On the third evening, Gul Jan came. I was sitting in my usual café, surrounded by hookah-smoking bravoes from the Black Mountain. An immense figure, shoulders like the side of a house, the traditional scar on his left cheek, and one shoulder bent with the weight of a lifetime's rifle-carrying, sat down beside me. As he shouted "*Ho Bacha*, bring pink tea!" I found a folded scrap of country-made paper being pressed into my hand.

Gul finished his cardamom tea in one gulp. Without looking at me he swaggered out, in the direction of the gunsmiths" bazaar, a snub Sten swinging idly from his belt.

Back in my apartment I read the message, with its cursive monogram of the Fakir. I was to go to the Frontier, "alone unarmed," to a point where Independent Territory bulges into Afghanistan.

Hiring a car for this ghastly jolting trip, I was there within eighteen hours. Under the shadow of a loaf-shaped rock in this defile miles from anywhere, an ancient shepherd sat. He took charge of the car, and asked to see what "Writing" I was carrying. I passed it to him. From behind the rock he produced a white cotton square, and laid it on the ground.

As the gloaming crept over the mountain glens, a posse of six Pathans rode up.

With the ends of their turbans held between their teeth in brigand style, they had the real air of freeborn Frontier men. In two minutes I was sitting, blindfolded, on their led-horse.

We plodded up stiff boulder-strewn gradients for an hour and a half. Then my eyes were uncovered. We were in a cup-shaped valley between the ranges, eerie in the light of the full moon.

Inside a long, low fort built against the narrow entrance to this depression, I lay down gratefully on a bare straw palliasse, and slept.

In spite of the sheepskin *postin* coat that covered me, the freezing cold woke me just before dawn streaked the sky. As I stirred, a guard in riding-boots, with bandoliers crossed over a leather jerkin, brought me pomegranate juice and hot water he had boiled over a charcoal fire.

I pulled aside the padded cotton curtain from the window's empty frame. All around the valley hoar frost gleamed over the vividly green turf. At one end a small wood carried a stream westward. On every side, where the cliffs rose sharply, grey granite buildings – creeper-clad in most cases – followed the contours of the rocks.

Several hundred men, fully armed, stood motionless, facing Meccaward at their daybreak prayer, their husky frames dwarfing the prayer-leader, a pace or two in front.

"*Rais-i-Jamhur*" ("President of the Republic"), said the guard.

This was my first glimpse of Mirza Haji Ali-Khan, the Fakir of Ipi.

Two men in fur caps, breeches and half-boots entered the guardhouse. In tunics which seemed to be modeled on the American type, they bore every indication of an organized military force. Embroidered shoulder-flashes carried the "Pushtunistan" insignia of a mountain with a sun rising behind it.

They introduced themselves as officers of the *élite* "old guard," recently formed from those Pathan guerrillas with Indian or Afghan army experience.

Major Asaf, one of the Fakir's retinue, had read an earlier book of mine, partly based on some of the Fakir's exploits. He shook me warmly by the hand. I believe that it was probably through him that I had my chance of seeing Gruik at all.

A Jeep – originally carried by human hands to the mountain stronghold – took me across the valley, past three anti-aircraft batteries, to the simple wooden house where the Fakir lives when he is "at home."

A radio mast protruded from the roof; green-dyed canvas draped the frame as camouflage against Pakistani reconnaissance planes. On the door, charmingly framed in a neat arabesque design, were inscribed the businesslike words: *Mirza Haji Ali-Khan, President of Free Pushtunistan.*

A six-footer with fixed bayonet presented arms as we approached. I eyed the grenade and sticks of explosive in his belt with some apprehension. Pathans are nothing if not careless about personal safety. Just inside the door stood the Fakir himself.

A slight, fair-skinned, brown-bearded man, he could easily pass for a European. He wore baggy trousers, chapli wrapped-over sandals, and an embroidered waistcoat over a military tunic.

"Welcome to Gruik." He took both my hands in his. "*Stare ma she!*" ("May you never be tired!") – the traditional Pathan greeting.

A fire burned in the large timbered room. On the walls maps of the neighboring countries were pinned, beside a revolver and a prayer-carpet hung on one side.

We sat down on bolsters, to share a breakfast of meat and yogurt, with tea from a charcoal-fed samovar.

The Fakir's eyes twinkled. He seemed so small, so delicately made, that I found it hard to believe that this was the most renowned warrior among a race of fighters.

"You are the first non-Pathan to come to Gruik. Not many even of our own people can get here: but I hope that before long things will be different."

One by one the rulers of this strange guerrilla State of three million people came on their morning visit to the Chief. I met

Mullah Sher Ali Khan, Advisor on National Defense, with a smart uniform under his sheepskin coat. He immediately spoke of "repeated aerial bombardments by Pakistan which have almost razed Gruik more than once."

"Those anti-aircraft guns were captured from them not far from Peshawar, in "49, and brought up here piece by piece."

At mid-morning I toured the arms factory, concealed in a honeycomb of caves tunneled out of the rock – probably prehistoric metal mines. Using electricity from wind-power, and sometimes hand-powered lathes, Afridi clansmen were laboriously turning out replicas of British Lee-Enfields. I picked one up. It was perfect, even to the monogram "GR" and a crown. But in addition were the words "FREE PUSHTUNISTAN."

A single light rocket gun on the principle of the "sobbing-sisters" weapon was shown to me as of a type under construction. In place of the batteries which ignited the projectile in the original model, this one seemed to be intended to work by some sort of flint and steel mechanism, not unlike a gas, cigarette lighter, butane lighter.

As each weapon was completed and tested, it was taken to the nearby range where recruits – some of them boys of fifteen or so – were being trained.

Claiming that the Fakir bore a charmed life, the Advisor showed me several bombs which, he said, had landed near him and which had failed to explode.

I was determined to get the story of Ipi's life. But he was reluctant to talk about himself. "I do not count," his small soft hands incessantly telling his rosary, "there is nothing unusual about me. I am forty-eight years old, was born in Khesora, in the center of the Free Land. My father was a holy man: that may be why I am now called the Fakir. I am a soldier, though I originally studied Islamic Law. When I had memorized the entire Qur'an, I turned to the study of modern Western science.

"For sixteen years I led Pathans against the Indo-British armies on the Frontier. I have never felt any rancor against Britain as such, of course – it was just my duty to help our people to hold their own. I used sometimes to spend periods in British India, and quite liked it."

The Fakir sighed. "I do not dislike the Pakistanis, either. But the British and I understood one another. I am sure that you will find thousands of people in England today who know this."

The fact that there was once a price of £6,000 on his head, and nobody ever claimed it, greatly amused him. "That was during the British days. I wonder whether the offer still holds?"

While his officers were without exception hard-bitten mountain fighters, the Fakir himself struck me again and again as strangely gentle, a dreamer who was only incidentally a soldier. His political acumen is famed. "We have no support of any kind from any outside power at all. We want to develop our country, and to guarantee its independent statehood. There are three million of us here, and several million more out by the border and now in what is called Pakistan. Many more are in Afghanistan. Our country has great mineral riches, and by any definition of international law we are sovereign in our own territory. Let us join the other nations as free men. This is one reason why our fighters went into Kashmir: to draw attention to our claims. As nothing was done, I called off almost all the Holy Warriors from the Kashmir Front." He spoke at length about alleged broken promises, and many more political matters.

I spent most of those three days touring the town and asking questions. Meanwhile the Fakir was busied in meeting delegations of tribal elders, leading the prayers and giving discourses.

The Minister of the Interior – Maulavi Zahir Shah, Khan – showed me the caverns, equipped with rations and beds, where the women and children sheltered during air raids.

In several discussions, the Fakir and his officers outlined their plans to me. Independent territory, they said, was becoming fairly well organized. Vendettas and the like had nearly been stopped. In the place of the blood-feud, the Fakir had instituted the Brotherhood Pact. Pakistan attacks, I was told, were designed to "contain" the Pathans, and prevent them from attacking Peshawar and other towns near the Border. But the Pathans claimed to be organizing for another reason. They had set up a National Assembly, and had a regular army. The "State" is short of money, and most revenue goes in arms and provisions. The Ipi espionage system extends throughout Afghanistan and Pakistan, where millions of Pathans live or work. Allegations that the Pathans were being helped by India were dismissed as "rubbish." "Do I eat the salt of the infidel, worshipper of sticks and stones?" roared the Fakir himself, when I spoke of this story I had heard in Karachi. His face was working, and he looked much more like a brigand chief at that moment.

Supplies such as gasoline and manufactured goods needed in the capital of Gruik and other parts of "Pushtunistan" are smuggled through the many small passes north and south of the Khyber, and probably also from well-wishers in Afghanistan.

The information service of the mountain capital is trying to get hold of a really powerful radio transmitter. At the present moment there are only a few small army sets in use.

Other communications are by carrier pigeon or couriers like Gul Khan.

Apart from the "Old Guard" veterans, several other formations exist. I watched some of the irregulars drilling under a Pathan former sergeant of the Khyber Rifles.

At one corner of the parade ground – which is also a hockey field for the AA guncrews – stands the war memorial. This takes the form of a grey stone slab: on it is cut the inscription in Pushtu and Arabic: "Remember them who were martyrs for your freedom, from before Alexander the Great, Until Allah Wills."

The rank and file of the guerrillas come nearer to the usual conception of a brigand chief plus pirate than anything I have seen elsewhere. Without exception they are armed to the teeth. The typical garb is high boots or sandals, baggy trousers, tunic shirt and tight-tied turban. This latter is also the warrior's shroud, and he carries it even when wearing a fur cap on the frozen mountain slopes. Military uniforms of every kind are greatly in vogue – but only "regular" troops may wear the copper badges with the mountain-and-sun emblem.

The general attitude of these Pathans is still that of the freebooter, the soldier-of-fortune. Few of them seem to care about the weightier implications of independent statehood. When I asked them about freedom, they usually replied that they were already free and always had been, as individuals. Their collective "war aims" are left to the Fakir and other leaders.

Perhaps the most surprising thing about this only guerrilla state in the world is that the Fakir has managed to get so many different clans to work together. For centuries these Afridis, Wazirs, Mohmands and the rest were at one another's throats. If this new unity stays, there is no knowing what new force may develop in No Man's Land.

Neither Afghanistan nor Pakistan rules the belt of territory running between their boundaries. Each country is interested in it as a frontier problem. Neither, so far, has officially recognized the Fakir and his Government. It will perhaps be a long time before either does so. In any case, the determination and persistence with which these Pathans are trying to form some sort of unified community amid the barren rocks of their homeland is something probably unique today.

The Fakir told me that he had received many offers from adventurers who wanted to join his ranks: but he would not say whether he had recruited any of them.

On the third day I was taken by another route out of the Pathan capital, with small gifts presented by the Fakir. One of them was a silver dagger inscribed Free Pushtunistan. Another was a red and green national flag, with the mountain and sunrise emblem embroidered on it in silk. Most of all I appreciated the Fakir's invitation to "Come again, when we have our complete freedom: then you will see what real hospitality is!"

Back in Kabul, people who heard that I had been to see the legendary Fakir treated me almost with apprehension. And there is no doubt that I was watched for the rest of my stay there by the odd idler who always seemed to be around. But I had met the Fakir of Ipi, and seen Pushtunistan in action. That was what mattered...

My self-imposed mission was ended: I could look back upon almost two years of wanderings, several tight corners, but a hundred-percent success score.

What had started out as a quest to see and record some of the world's remaining challenges of the East had, by its very success, whetted my appetite for more.

I sat down in Kabul's biting winter to write up my notes. My never-failing companion lay beside me. Until my wanderings were due to start again, Robot f/2.8 lay snugly in its case.

* * *

A Request

If you enjoyed this book, please review it on Amazon and Goodreads.

Reviews are an author's best friend.

To stay in touch with news on forthcoming editions of Idries Shah works, please sign up for the mailing list:

 http://bit.ly/ISFlist

And to follow him on social media, please go to any of the following links:

 https://twitter.com/idriesshah

 https://www.facebook.com/IdriesShah

 http://www.youtube.com/idriesshah999

 http://www.pinterest.com/idriesshah/

 http://bit.ly/ISgoodreads

 http://idriesshah.tumblr.com

http://idriesshahfoundation.org

Lightning Source UK Ltd.
Milton Keynes UK
UKOW02f0635270416

273052UK00003BA/36/P